Training
Student
Library Staff

Dr. Lesley S. J. Farmer

Linworth Publishing, Inc.
Worthington, Ohio

Library of Congress Cataloging-in-Publication Data

Farmer, Leslie S.J.
    Training student library staff / by Leslie S.J. Farmer.
       p. cm. -- (Professional growth series)
     ISBN 0-938865-56-0 (perfect bound)
     1. School libraries--United States--Personnel management. 2. Student library assistants--Training of--United States.
  I. Title. II. Series.
  Z675.S3F238   1997
  023'.3--dc21   96-51148
                                                 CIP

Published by Linworth Publishing, Inc.
480 East Wilson Bridge Road, Suite L
Worthington, Ohio 43085

Copyright © 1997 by Linworth Publishing, Inc.

Series Information:
  From the Professional Growth Series

ISBN 0-938865-56-0

5 4 3 2 1

Table of Contents

Introduction

Students are our business, our only business.

The information and service that libraries provide are for the betterment of young people. Not surprisingly, then, the effective use of library student staff offers a wonderful opportunity to model library instruction and student participation. It also signals the need for thoughtful preparation as librarians train young people to carry out the library's mission.

The first chapter of this book lays the groundwork for training staff effectively. Until the librarian determines the main functions of the library within the school, she or he cannot thoughtfully assign meaningful duties to the library's aides. The librarian must also possess good management and supervisory skills in order to make best use of student staff—and have them enjoy their work. Theory and practical applications are blended to provide contextual guidance in these processes.

The second chapter of the book provides outlines for training sessions. Each one includes activity description, objectives, process, demonstration ideas, student activities, follow-up, and evaluation. Training is grouped into seven major library functions or services, with an introductory page delineating the critical features of the common characteristics for each group of tasks.

By melding guiding principles and practical lessons, school librarians can provide their library student staff with the grounding needed to carry out the library's mission and support individual student growth.

Chapter 1

Foundations of Using Student Library Staff

Assessing the Library's Needs

A school. Teachers. Students. *And* the library. Whether it's called a resource room, a media information center, "information central," or a school library, the basic mission of the library media program is "to ensure that students and staff are effective users of ideas and information." (AASL 1)

That's a tall order. Certainly, the school librarian could live in the library and work non-stop every day every hour, and still have work to do. Certainly, the school librarian could use good help in order to get that work done. However, to provide the best service in the most effective way, the school librarian needs to look at the site's mission and match it with its potential staff. Only by determining the overall context of the library can meaningful staff contributions be made.

Developing a mission statement

What is the "business" of the school library? Why does it exist? What is its niche? Here are some possibilities:

- A resource center to support school curriculum
- A facilitator for lifelong learning
- A haven for reflective thinking and interaction with great thinkers
- A production center for creating means to share ideas
- A staff development resource center
- A gateway to worldwide sources
- A place that encourages reading
- A source for information leading to solutions for personal issues
- An aesthetic feast
- A referral institution for survival needs
- A literacy center
- An access point for educational technology
- A means to individualize learning and learning plans
- A career exploration center
- A safe place to hide out and get "centered"

All of these missions are within the realm of the school library. It is the school librarian's job to prioritize these potential missions, and decide how they are aligned with the school's mission. It is important to remember that no single entity can fill all the demands and wishes of all its potential clientele. The library should determine its unique resources and contributions and its context within the school's total program. This task of determining and articulating the school library's mission needs to be done in a collaborative and consensual manner that includes the input of students, staff, parents, and community. When all of the potential users buy into the vision, then they will experience a greater sense of ownership—and will help the school librarian carry out the mission.

Such an approach typically takes more time than if the school librarian were to come up with a mission statement independently. The issue, though, is relevance and "connectivity." The school librarian will find greater support if the plan is the result of community-wide involvement; how can one object to a plan that one chose? For example, if a school board of trustees approves a school library's long-range plan, then that body of authority is compelled to provide the financial and structural support to enable that action plan to be implemented.

Needs Assessment

The first step in such involvement is a needs assessment. What perceived needs are articulated by all potential constituents? The assessment may be keyed into the school's mission statement. It may be aligned with existing district direction. There should be some accountable "handle," whatever the framework for the assessment. In order to create a rich and accurate picture, a variety of assessors and assessment tools should be incorporated.

In line with the above framework, examining school documents is a good starting assessment task. What are the school's principles and policies? What student outcomes are expected? What curricular and co-curricular programs are offered? What personnel competencies and standards exist? Does the district or state have overarching mandates?

Representatives of all constituent groups should be involved: a heterogeneous group of students, faculty, staff, administrators, and parents. By grouping assessors along both cross-demographic and within-group samples, the librarian can get different types of information. For example, students with like interests may lobby for a particular library emphasis. A widely mixed focus group may provide across-the-board consensus on basic issues. In fact, a study of the demographics of the population to be served is a necessary part of the assessment.

Likewise, a variety of assessment tools can offer insights along different dimensions. The school community can rank the relative importance of a standard list of library services and resources. Output measures can quantify reference fill rates. Open-ended questionnaires can elicit opinions not brought up formally. Focus group discussions offer a chance for ideas to bounce back and forth. Concurrently, thoughtful observation by the librarian can also reveal significant needs.

As the school community provides input in various ways, their wants and needs must be articulated and differentiated. Students may *want* to be able to gamble or swim in the library, but such preferences aren't very feasible. In a more technological vein, students may want all state-of-the-art multimedia computers, but the school's finances might well prohibit such an investment, particularly if the rest of the school have no computers at all. Teachers might not think that the librarian *needs* to be an instructional partner, although the professional literature recommends such a role—and students yearn for expert guidance. If the community thinks that a particular need is vital, though, the librarian should listen to that need and address it; value judgments seriously affect library programs. So if a librarian dislikes storytelling, but the school highly values that function within the library, then the librarian should consider having other adults or *student staff* trained and available to provide that service.

Another important part of the needs process is assessing the resources available. Such an inventory helps determine both the reason for needs as well as the ability to meet those needs. For example, if students need science reference tools, then an assessment of available resources in that area is required. If an overall direction is desirable, all types of resources should be examined: material (print and nonprint information, equipment, supplies), facilities (space, furniture, lighting and heat, traffic flow, outlets, cables and lines), financial (budget, donations, gifts in kind), and human (professional, paraprofessional, adult and student volunteers). Staff time, largely over-looked, should probably be considered one of these resources.

Part of the needs assessment should also address how well the library is *meeting* those needs. The assessment instrument should include a ranking for satisfaction as well as for importance. By examining the relative impor-tance of a library function, and the degree and quality at which it is being done, the librarian can shape the program. For instance, if the need for fictional reading is high, and the school community is satisfied with the library's collection, then the library is on the right track. However, if the population is *not* satisfied, then one of two factors may be involved: a poor or inappropriate collection or lack of knowledge about the library's holdings.

The librarian must be able to ferret out the reason for any gaps in needs satisfaction. Basically, either the library has to change, or the librarian must change the community's perceptions. Note that external forces beyond the librarian's control influence the library program: facility constraints, changing student demographics, a sizeable estate donation to the library. Obviously, the librarian should identify those forces and take advantage of those cases when they impact positively.

In the final analysis, the librarian has to examine all of the data in light of current library practice, school directives, and available resources. That interpretation should answer the central question: "What should the library be providing?"

Strategic Planning and Staffing Needs

Out of the needs and resources come the library's mission statement, its guiding principles. With that mission in mind, the librarian can now plan how to achieve its potential. The strategic plan makes the mission real; it specifies the library's resources, the institutional and community support, the potential clientele and users, and the potential opportunities and risks.

Different climates call for different strategies. For instance, in a stable school environment, the strategic plan can be well detailed. Where the school is undergoing major reform, the strategic plan needs to be more flexible. In unstable conditions, the strategic plan may need a backup direction in order to implement needed library functions.

What are some variations in strategy planning?

- A *stability* strategy endeavors to maintain the status quo. It is largely a management issue, and focuses on smooth operations. This kind of strategy is appropriate for environments that are doing well and do not anticipate change in staffing or student demographics.
- A *growth* strategy is called upon when the student population or financial opportunity is increasing. In some cases, a growth strategy signals a change in library staffing where there is a possibility for greater library use or services. A growth strategy is also appropriate when a school is trying to increase its enrollment or improve its reputation.
- A *retrenchment* strategy is needed when budgets or other resources are substantially reduced. The concept is to minimize the negative affects of the cutbacks.
- A *focus* strategy aims to establish a niche for the library in the school. Perhaps the library wants to exploit its advantage as an information center; perhaps it wants to emphasize its leadership in individualized learning opportunities. In this kind of strategy planning, the key is to find a unique service and specialized resources that support such a service.

One way to approach this task is to develop a planning diagram that details the specific objective (or group of objectives), a timeline to accomplish those objectives, a designation of where those objectives are to be accomplished, and who will be responsible for developing and implementing the strategic plan. A good idea is to create a group of planning diagrams that coordinate the different detailed objectives. The librarian can reorganize these plans in terms of each aspect: objective, master timeline, location, and personnel. Here is an example:

Objective	Timeline	Location	Person Responsible
Students use CD-ROMs independently		library	librarian, teachers, aides
1. library staff learn CD-ROM	Sep. 1-5	library	librarian, staff, aides
2. library staff teach peers	Sep. 8-12	library	librarian, staff, aides
3. produce guidesheet/aid	Sep. 1-19	library	librarian, staff, aides
4. create student lesson	Sep. 22-26	library, class	librarian, teacher
5. conduct learning activity	Oct. 1-2	library	school community

This kind of plan can be used to describe overarching functions as well as specific ongoing tasks:

Objective	Timeline	Location	Person Responsible
Display books	weekly	display case	student aide
1. choose theme	Thursday		
2. choose books	Thursday		
3. make sign	Friday		
4. put up display	Monday		

As the librarian compiles these plans, priorities arise. By knowing what resources are available, the librarian can determine staffing needs and patterns. While paid staff usually can't change, the utilization of student aides can fluctuate. With thoughtful planning, the librarian can make use of existing aides and recruit new people with intriguing projects.

Policies and Procedures

Because each staff member represents the library, policies and procedures should be in place—and clear to all involved. These guidelines constitute the basis for decision-making, so they need to be complete and accurate. Usually the librarian has those policies in mind, but if they are not written and available to staff members, the staff will either ask the librarian continuously for advice or will devise their own, sometimes contradictory, policies and procedures.

The set of guiding documents can be divided into three categories.
- *Descriptions* delineate a local situation, such as clientele demographics.
- *Policies* are philosophical statements of intent that provide the basis for decision-making.
- *Procedures* list the steps required to perform a specific task. Usually, few policies are needed. Good policies, mainly statements developed by the American Library Association, already exist. Others are generated from state codes and regulations, such as education codes, and serve as legal prescriptions.

The usual set of policies includes a code of ethics, and a position statement on evaluation, selection, donations, copyright, controversial materials and access, conservation, and discarding. Additional policies may address issues of professional growth and instruction. Policies for circulation, fund-raising, solicitations, facilities, resources sharing, programs, community relations, and production are usually very individualized to suit local needs.

Procedures also tend to be site-specific. Moreover, they are more apt to be developed with the full cooperation of the library staff. As tasks are carried out, changes in methods and sequencing can improve the outcome. In fact, most policies are written over time as a need arises or school operations change. Procedures can be even more fluid as the library adopts new technology or changing school philosophies. Furthermore, student staff should be encouraged to suggest ways to modify procedures to provide better service as they come up with better solutions to library operational problems. This ongoing collaborative approach to procedures builds staff ownership as well as acknowledges thoughtful change.

Of course, all established policies must be followed and enforced or they lose their usefulness. As they reflect professional practice, policies provide a frame of reference for good library service. Even policies need to be reviewed occasionally to insure their validity, however, so the librarian should check on all documentation each year.

The following outline provides a framework for organizing a manual of descriptions ("d"), policies ("p"), and procedures ("r") that reflect the library's mission and needs:

I. Mission statement d

II. Administration
   A. Governance d
   B. Personnel d (p for credential policy)
   C. Budget and funding d p
   D. Documentation and record-keeping d p
   E. Code of ethics p

III. Facilities
   A. Site d
   B. Furniture d
   C. Equipment d
   D. Use of facilities p r
   E. Disasters p r

IV. Acquisitions of materials
   A. Evaluation p r
   B. Selection p r
   C. Ordering d
      1. Solicitations p
      2. Standing orders r
   D. Donations p r
   E. Receipt r
   F. Resource sharing p r

V. Processing of materials
   A. Classification r
   B. Cataloging r
   C. Bibliographic control and access p r
      1. Databases r
      2. Interlibrary loan p r
   D. Physical processing r

VI. Organization and use of materials
   A. Organization r
      1. Special collections d p r
      2. Remote collections d p r
   B. Circulation p r
   C. Copyright p
   D. Maintenance
      1. Conservation p r
      2. Inventory r
   E. Discarding p r
   F. Controversial materials p r

VII. Services
- A. Instruction p r
- B. Programs p r
- C. Production and duplication p r
- D. Communication d
- E. Community relations p r
- F. Professional growth p
    1. Training r
    2. Development r
    3. Networking d
- G. Fund-raising p r

Writing Good Documentation

Writing clear policies and procedures may seem like a daunting task, but training each library staff member individually every task quickly becomes tedious and time-intensive. A well-written manual of procedures explains itself, and makes it easier for staff to understand and perform library tasks successfully. Library staff can even laminate individual sheets as reference guides alongside their workstation. If the resultant manual is placed in a binder, updates and revisions will be easy to do.

The librarian does not have to re-invent every policy or procedure. Taking ideas from peers and professional organizational publications not only saves time but can represent the best thinking on particular topics. For example, the American Library Association and its divisions have policy statements on access to information (including technological sources), collection development, the role of the school library specialist, and intellectual freedom. States and districts often have codes on issues such as donations, withdrawals, personnel, and safety. Commercial companies may supply procedural guidelines on such tasks as checkouts and cataloging. Some specific procedural examples are provided in the lesson plans section of this book.

Still, the librarian will need to create some original policies and procedures. The guiding principle in writing procedures is to use simple, specific directions:

- Write one concept or one task per page, so that staff can refer to just the information needed at the moment.
- Explain all technical terms.
- If computer commands are involved, list them separately and note their use.
- Number each step.
- Write all the possible actions at steps where decisions are required.
- Give an example of each format used, with possible responses for each each action within each format.
- Leave nothing to guesswork. Particularly if the procedure involves computer inputting, consistent spelling and spacing are required to avoid complications. Include diagrams and illustrations when appropriate (such as drymounting techniques).

- Catch the reader's eye with graphic devices: indentions, <u>underlines</u>, *italics*, **boldface**, and • bullets or *asterisks.
- Explain what to do if staff make a mistake. Help them correct the error—or get back to the start.

Other media, such as cassette tapes and videotapes, may be produced as procedural guides. As the steps are described on tape, the staff member can try out the action. Staff can stop or rewind tapes to reinforce learning. This approach is especially useful for the poor reader, but requires more effort for the librarian to create.

Whatever the format, all documentation needs to be tested before the copy is finalized. Student staff should follow the directions, with the librarian present to observe and ask questions.

- Do staff understand all the terminology?
- What questions do they ask?
- Can they perform the tasks independently?
- What modifications do they suggest?

Such testing takes time—and is worth it. Clear, self-explanatory documentation saves the librarian many hours by reducing the number of times procedures must be demonstrated. And the positive experience enables library staff to work more autonomously and productively.

School Context

Imagine your school as a target, complete with concentric circles and numerical values. Where would your library dart land: in the center or near the edge? How much would the library be worth?

Usually one of the goals of the school library is to become the hub of the school, where learning is centered. But just as a hub has to connect with each and every spoke in order to keep the whole mechanism running smoothly, so too does the library have to keep centered in its mission and be well connected to the rest of the school community. The library must be aligned with the school in order to serve it well. Only in knowing what is happening in the rest of the school can the library enrich and complement existing programs—and develop its own unique contributions. This awareness facilitates two-way partnerships, where the library can become a powerful change agent for education. This chapter explores this symbiotic relationship, especially as it impacts student staff.

Culture

Underlying the operations of the school is the school culture: a set of norms and expectations that prescribe acceptable behavior. Sometimes it is commmunicated formally through documented rules and policies; sometimes it is tacitly conveyed in staff lounge interactions. For some schools, the prevailing culture is well-defined and known; for others it is hard to discern. But even an apparent lack of culture indicates a certain belief.

So, too, the library manifests a mini-culture. For the library to be effective, it should either reflect or drive the total school's culture; otherwise, the misalignment between library and the rest of the school can cause frustration.

Several components of school culture follow:
- Student profile:
  What are the socioeconomic backgrounds of the students?
  What geographic areas are represented by the student population?
  If the school is not a neighborhood institution, transportation and volunteer patterns, among other issues, will be affected. What do students value: grades, money, friends, sports, effort?
  How homogeneous is the student population?
  How tolerant are students to those outside the norm?
  Who are the popular and powerful students? What groups do they represent?
  What kind of influence do students have in school matters?
  What postsecondary options do students typically pursue?
  Work, junior college, university, Ivy League, travel?

- Community profile:
  What careers and values do students' community parents represent?
  What role do parents play in the school?
  What kind of support or opposition do parents present?
  What are the characteristics of the school's neighborhood?
  What is the relationship between the school and the community?

Who are the key players in the community?

What are their relationships with the school?

How does the community influence curricular, co-curricular, and career exploration activities?

- Faculty profile:

What socioeconomic backgrounds do the faculty represent?

What are the educational backgrounds of faculty?

What is the favored teaching and classroom management style?

How do faculty relate to students? Are teachers called by first or last name, for instance?

How do faculty related to administration?

How do faculty typically group themselves: by discipline, age, geographic area, personality?

To what extent is team planning and teaching done?

How effective is it?

What are the characteristics of social encounters? formal school events, TGIF gatherings, coffee breaks, mail room chats, off-site parties?

To what extent do faculty socialize?

Who holds power, both formal and informal, within the faculty? What is the basis of power?

How are teachers evaluated?

- Academic profile:

What is the school's mission? Is it a comprehensive institution or a magnet content-specific school?

What curriculum is offered?

How is it developed and modified?

What are the academic expectations?

What is the relative importance of academics, co-curricular activities, school-to-work, and social life?

What are the yearly and daily schedules?

What block or modular schedules exist?

How are students counseled?

What opportunities are given for staff development?

- Governance profile:

How are decisions made?

What are the spoken and unspoken rules?

Who enforces them?

What is the role of administration?

What is the relationship between the school and its district?

Climate Implications for School Library Staff

Within the school, the school library has its own culture. Moreover, each library staff member represents certain norms, so the librarian needs to transmit those expectations to the student library staff. Some generic principles beyond specific school cultures apply to most libraries. Most have:

- An atmosphere of learning
- Respect for all library users
- Respect for ideas
- A helpful attitude and sense of service.

However, different school cultural "codes" call for different strategies within the library. Staff should be sensitive to these norms and carry them out in the library. Librarians should treat student staff accordingly, and teach them to behave within those cultural expectations. Here are some examples:

- Student characteristics:

    If many students are non-native speakers, then student staff should represent those languages spoken.

    If students come from a distance, then fewer student staff will probably be available before and after school.

    If student government is strong, then student staff should also play an important role in library decisions.

- Community characteristics:

    If most families are two-income households, then there will probably be fewer parent volunteers; student staff will play a bigger role.

    If the public library has close ties with the school library, then greater opportunities will probably exist for student internships and job shadowing.

    If businesses support the library, then student staff may have more resources available to learn to use.

- Faculty characteristics:

    If faculty work independently and don't team up with librarians much, then student staff may become the chief communication link.

    If faculty work closely and informally with students, then the librarian should reflect that same kind of informality.

    If teachers are evaluated by students, then the librarian should be evaluated by the student staff as well.

- Academic characteristics:

    If students are grade-oriented, then grades will probably be a major assessment tool of student staff.

    If clubs are popular, then a library club may be the most effective way to recruit and structure student staff.

    If most students are planning to enter college directly after graduation, then research strategies may constitute a major part of student staff training.

- Governance characteristics:

    If the school is highly centralized, then student staffing and training may be standardized.

    If group participation is highly prized, then student staff should meet regularly to review and modify library practice.

    If rules are usually made, then student staff should know library policies well—and probably help shape library rules.

Curriculum

The customary way for schools to structure their mission to prepare students for the real world is through curricular offerings, so curriculum issues typically drive the library program. In terms of student library staff, curriculum affects practice in three ways: structuring student staffing and assessment; teaching skills that student staff need to have; and providing appropriate resources with which student staff work.

Structuring student staff: In some schools library service is offered as a formal class. The goals for such a course may vary greatly. Library work may serves as a school-to-work option, it may be used to help students polish information literacy skills, or it may follow a teacher aide or intern model. Whatever the objectives, students sign up hoping to reach those goals. The one drawback to a formal course with credit attached is that a student may take the class just to satisfy graduation requirement hours; the librarian then sometimes has a harder job engaging the student so that the work becomes a meaningful experience. Assessment varies with the course objective to some degree. If the emphasis is on future preparation, then the librarian needs to examine the student's potential to learn and succeed independently. In some cases, following directions may comprise a significant portion of the assessment. If workplace skills are being emphasized, then interpersonal relations may be a factor in evaluating performance.

Instruction: In traditional school curricula, instruction is given in daily "doses" for about an hour a day, including time to practice the skill. As credit numbers vary, so the number of class contact hours varies; for instance, if library service is a two-credit course, then the student would probably work two hours weekly. In an intern model, all library student staff might meet one hour a week for formal instruction, and carry out their tasks throughout the week whenever they had scheduled time. Depending on the course objectives, students might learn clerical skills such as filing and word processing or they might learn college-preparatory skills such as research strategies and database management. Instructional delivery methods may also differ—from formal lecture to self-paced workbooks, from peer demonstrations to commercial videotapes.

Resources: The overall curricular emphasis also affects the materials that student staff use. If curriculum is textbook-based, library student staff might focus on leisure reading materials and activities. If resource-based learning is the school's focus, then staff will need to work with a variety of reference sources. If teachers are encouraged to use a variety of media to engage different learning styles, then the library staff is likely to learn how to operate equipment and production tools.

Getting into Activity Mode

Co-curricular activities comprise another important connection for libraries. One approach is to provide programs and interest groups that extend the library. Another strategy is to build on the co-curricular efforts of other school entities.

In some schools a library club or co-curricular activity may be offered. Membership is typically self-selective, so students of like mind are more likely to attend. These members usually have a passion about libraries—or books or whatever resources are prevalent. As a club or co-curricular option, library service takes on a social nature as well. Students are likely to spend as much time developing friendships and hosting events as they are learning library skills. The social aspect can work well for those libraries wanting a strong programming or public relations component; the library club can plan and run those projects under the general guidance of the librarian. Book or film discussion groups, storytelling "guilds," and video news programs fall under this activities umbrella.

In some schools, library service is considered a community service option; such an approach usually attracts two kinds of students: those who like to help people in general, and those who prefer one-time projects. Sometimes honor societies require student service hours; the librarian has the benefit of bright students who would normally not have the time to commit themselves to long-term library assistance.

The library can also link with other school activities that students work on. A recycling club can pick up old library newspapers and computer printouts. The library can host multicultural club or poetry group presenters. Student aides who work with peers having several physical challenges can use the library to tutor or to find books for their charges to enjoy.

Giving Credit to the Library Staff

Sometimes student library staff can earn credit and grades for their work. As credit guidelines are established, school precedence needs to be considered. Library credit usually follow the structure of Carnegie units, which designate the number of required teacher-student contact hours. Sometimes, variable credit may be given, depending upon the number of days that the student works in the library. Additionally, credit for library staff may be deemed academic or nonacademic, depending upon the nature of the course and the presecse of similar course offerings throughout the school. Library staff may earn pass-fail credit, or may receive A-F grades, depending on the librarian's and school's expectations and negotiations. In some cases, students may have the option of choosing what kind of credit and grading scale they wish to use.

Of course, library grading policies also should be in line with the rest of the school's practices. If the goal of the course is to learn academic skills, then grades should reflect scholarship demands. If the course follows a technical avenue, then performance levels should be in alignment with similar tech prep offerings. If the library staff act as teacher's aides, then their efforts—and grades—should mirror the productivity that librarian counterparts expect. For student office workers, attitude and attendance may count as much as product; if library staff hold the same status, then they should be evaluated similarly.

Whatever credit and grading policy options are used, the librarian should set forth those expectations clearly at the beginning. Having ground rules makes it easier for students to comply with them—and helps the librarian get straying students back on task. The following rubric shows one way to evaluate student behaviors.

Rubric For Grading:

A: Fully accomplishes the purpose of the task
- Student work shows full grasp and use of library central concepts and processes.
- Student works efficiently, accurately, and independently without supervision.
- Student consistently arrives on time and stays on task.
- Student consistently shows willingness to learn and help.
- Student consistently works well with adults and students.

B: Substantially accomplishes the purpose of the task
- Student work shows essential grasp and use of library central concepts and processes.
- Student generally works efficiently and accurately with little supervision.
- Student generally arrives on time and stays on task.
- Student generally shows willingness to learn and help.
- Student generally works well with adults and students.

C: Partially accomplishes the purpose of the task
- Student work shows partial but limited grasp of library central concepts and processes.
- Student works adequately but needs some supervision.
- Student sometimes arrives late and is sometimes distracted.
- Student occasionally shows unwillingness to learn and help.
- Student works adequately with adults and students.

D: Makes little or no progress in accomplishing the purpose of the task
- Student work shows little or no grasp of library central concepts and processes.
- Student works inefficiently and needs constant supervision.
- Student has excessive absences or tardies.
- Student does not stay on task.
- Student is seldom willing to learn or help.
- Student does not work well with adults and students.

F: Makes no progress or undermines the purpose of the task
- Student shows no grasp of any library concepts or processes.
- Student does not work, even under constant supervision.
- Student has excessive absences and tardies.
- Student never stays on task.
- Student is never willing to learn or help.
- Student disrupts or harrasses adults or students.

Connecting with the Rest of the Staff

As important as library resources and programs are, effective interaction between the library staff and the rest of the school is imperative if the library is to carry out its mission. The librarian needs to provide a model for good communication, and must instill this behavior in the student library staff. A good place to practice appropriate interaction is within the library, with both paid staff and volunteers. Some tips follow:

- Offer a vision of the library that is inspiring and meaningful.
- Get to know staff on a one-to-one basis. Take individual differences into account when assigning duties. Promote mutual respect and trust.
- Educate the staff not only in terms of the library but of the entire school.
- Enable staff rather than control them.
- Share information.
- Encourage broad-based decision-making.

How well do the library student staff network with the rest of the school to promote the library? The more effective their personal and library skills in working with others, the greater the benefits for the staff—and library service. Here are a dozen guiding questions:

- Are student staff acquainted with the library software and equipment that is replicated elsewhere in the school?
- Can student staff recommend good library books and nonprint resources to others?
- Do student staff learn skills from other teachers that can be applied to library work, such as computer technology, writing, or artistry?
- Do student staff conduct inservice workshops for peers or faculty about computer-related subjects?
- Do student staff make flyers, name tags, or banners for the school?
- Do student staff troubleshoot equipment use for peers and faculty?
- Do student staff design inhouse databases for administrative or curriculum purposes?
- Do student staff create or maintain Web pages for school?
- Do student staff help peers and teachers with Internet searches? Do they create bookmarks to valuable Web sites?
- Do student staff maintain school electronic bulletin boards?
- Do student staff create displays or bulletin boards about the library in other parts of the school?
- Do student staff handle library-sponsored food fair or carnival booths at school events?

The more that the librarian empowers library staff, the more important will be the role of the library as a whole.

Safety First

Safety is an underlying issue for the librarian. Too often the librarian does not consider possible safety hazards. Yet all staff are responsible for assuring a safe environment for learning. Thus, it is up to the librarian to teach both student and adult staff members the safe way to work. The most effective approach is one of prevention: providing a safe environment. The second step is dealing with unsafe situations. Emphasis should be placed on the proactive, preventive approach. Librarians should tackle the following safety issues, and teach safe practices to all staff members from the start. A safe beginning prevents unhappy crises later.

Probably the most significant factor in safety is good judgment. Student staff need careful watching and guidance. They should engage in library work that is appropriate to their maturity and capability. Moreover, they should be taught the safety features for whatever task they perform, from shelving (e.g., how to move a cart) to videotaping (e.g., wrapping the cord around the tripod to avoid yanking out the line).

Librarians should also know current school safety policies and practices. Each school has an emergency plan and safety equipment, which the librarian should know and train the staff on. Students should know what to report, and should practice the buddy system if they have to leave the library (go in pairs, so if one has a problem, the other one can report back).

Facilities: The library should be easily accessible to all students and staff, including those with disabilities. It should be free of obvious hazards, and have at least two exits. First aid equipment should be handy and in good shape. Student staff should know the followings skills:
- How to keep the library clean
- What to do in an emergency
- How to transport physically challenged students
- How to assist with simple first aid.

Supervision: The library should be supervised by an adult whenever students are present. In some schools, the adult must be a certificated teacher. When a student staff member leaves the library, she or he should notify the supervisor. In many settings, the student needs a hall pass so other people know that the student is on official business.

Equipment: All equipment should be in good working order and secured in safe locations. Manufacturer instructions for safe use and care of equipment should be read and kept available for easy reference. Electrical outlets should be adequate for equipment needs, and grounded. Safety equipment, (e.g., fire extinguishers, flashlight, radio), should be easily accessible. Student staff should follow these safe practices:
- Check equipment before using it; report any defective equipment immediately.
- Plug and unplug equipment at the plug itself; don't yank the cord.
- Coil up cords safely.
- Lift equipment and other heavy objects safely, bending at the knees instead of at the small of the back.
- Transport equipment safely; if a cart is used, be sure to secure the equipment on it.
- Know how to use equipment before using it; ask for directions.
- Store tools and supplies in their proper place when finished with them.

Emergencies: Be prepared for emergencies and disasters. For instance:
- During lightning storms, stay away from doors, windows, plumbing, and electrical equipment.
- During winter storms, check battery-powered equipment such as flashlights and radios.
- During floods, turn off electrical equipment (and let adults unplug them).
- During earthquakes, duck under heavy furniture or stand in a doorway; stay away from windows.

Harassment and other unsafe advances: Student staff should feel safe and secure in the library. If they think they are being harassed or put in an unsafe situation, they should report the action immediately to adult staff, preferably the librarian. Potential unsafe behaviors include, among others:

- Verbal or physical threats, harassment, or abuse
- Criminal attempts, such as theft or destruction of property
- Public exposure
- Unsafe activity, such as tipping equipment or jostling people

In general, all library activities should be planned and implemented so as to guarantee the well-being of the library student staff. Adults and students need to follow proper safety practices at all times.

Keep it Legal

The library staff must also be aware of legal issues: copyright, privacy, censorship, school regulations, union issues, civil rights. The librarian is accountable for the staff, including students. Thus, knowledge about varied possible legal breaches should constitute part of the librarian's job. Here are some of the legal practices that need to be passed on to the student library staff:

- Circulation records are confidential. Students should not say who has checked out a specific resource. Nor should students write comments in the circulation program about others.
- Student staff must follow copyright law. For instance, they should not copy software illegally. The librarian may ask student staff to copy a disk to keep as an archive copy of a program, depending on the producer's agreement, but that copying procedure must be made very clear to the student.
- Harassment and discrimination are illegal; student staff must treat all people in the library courteously and respectfully.
- Students must follow all governmental laws. Theft, destruction of property, non-medicinal drug use, and forgery are just some of the possible criminal acts that student staff could possibly be arrested for.
- Students must follow all school rules and regulations.

While this list looks forbidding, and perhaps unrealistic, every one of these legal issues has been breached by library student staff. If expectations—and consequences—relative to legal action are made clear from the beginning, student staff will be more likely to be law-abiding citizens.

Assessing the Student Library Staff

"Hi, I'm George. I've been assigned to work here in the library."

What's your first reaction: Who is this kid? Thank goodness for competent help! What am I supposed to do with him? Why is the library a dumping ground for misfits? Is she good at computer troubleshooting?

Long before the first library student staff girl or boy crosses the library's threshhold, the librarian should have an idea of what that student can do. Student help can further the library substantially, though young people should not take the place of paid staff. Furthermore, the school library should benefit the student, offering her or him a meaningful learning environment. Rather than dealing with each student on an ad hoc basis, the librarian should determine the roles and functions of library student staff in general. Once those policy-based expectations are clarified, it is easier to assess the capabilities and interests of each student and to match those characteristics with the library's situation.

The Role of the Student Library Staff

The role of library student staff depends on the school library's mission and present staffing. *Information Powers'* mission can be used as a beginning point. If the library's program "ensures that students and staff are effective users of ideas and information" (AASL 1), then student staffing can be established to:

- Train a core of students to become effective users and act as models for other students.
- Provide greater physical access to materials through more staffing for circulation and timely storage and retrieval (filing and shelving).
- Provide greater access to information through student research aid (database retrieval).
- Provide greater intellectual access to materials through peer instruction and communication.
- Encourage reading through student staff reviewing, storytelling, and display work.
- Model effective instructional design principles and activities through staff training.

The more clearly articulated the mission, the easier it is to recruit student staff who will carry out that mission. Ideally, student staff should be comprised of motivated students who believe in the library's mission and want to be part of that action. It should be noted that the library's reputation or image probably speaks louder than the written mission. For example, if the school library's mission is to encourage reading, but it's known as a good place to "hang out" and play with computers, guess which kind of student staff will probably volunteer: the bookworm or the social hacker?

The school library usually has a basic philosophy about its staff, which generally reflects its mission. For instance, if the library's mission is to facilitate lifelong learning, then the following practices would be expected:

- Opportunities to explore librarianship as a profession
- Ongoing staff development for both student and adult staff
- Inclusion of adult volunteers both to train and to be trained by students and other adults.

If the library's mission is to serve as an access point for educational technology, then staffing might include these characteristics:

- Screening of staff to ensure a basic competence in the use of educational technology
- Heavy-duty training on equipment use and troubleshooting
- Tiered or specialized staffing patterns based on student level of expertise (some students would not be involved in technology, some would manage basic automated circulation operations, some would word process, some would install program, and some would repair hardware).

Again, if the staffing patterns accurately manifest the library's mission, then it is more likely that like-minded students will volunteer to help.

Note that the role of the student library staff, while it focuses on the library's needs, must be determined in light of the student's own needs relative to the rest of the school.

Regardless of the library's mission, the librarian must remember that students are, first and foremost, young persons. They have developmental needs, they want to make friends with their peers, and they want to act their age. Thus, teenagers don't want strangulating structure and arbitrary rules; they want to help fashion their role. Simultaneously, they should not be put in a situation where they feel unduly responsible, such as managing a lab or being in charge of substantial money matters. Even junior high staff want some responsibility, such as checking out materials, but work better with more defined rules and limitations than at the high school level.

Furthermore, student library staff have school responsibilities which must be respected. Occasionally, a student feels more at home in the library than in any other part of the school, and may want to help all the time. Since the school librarian *is* a teacher, she or he should help the student become more involved with the rest of schooling rather than hide in the library. In an effort to get involved in school as an entering freshman, some students sign up to help in the library, only to find that they didn't realize the amount of time needed to manage more demanding academic workloads. The librarian should be sensitive to those realizations and help the student "save face" about cutting down on library staff hours. On the other hand, the student staff person who takes advantage of his or her position and gossips about circulation records or fines should be told about students' right to privacy and confidentiality.

Thus, student library staff function on two levels: They act as representatives of the student body, and they reflect the school library as they assist in carrying out the library's mission. This duality can be a real asset to the librarian. Student staff can provide valuable input from the users' point of view. They can suggest popular reading material, and keep the librarian current on student trends and issues. Likewise, student library staff can help relay the library's message to the rest of the school. Indeed, student staff are the library's greatest Public Relation agents.

Within this general construct, the staff program should allow students to help delineate their specific roles. Ideally, a steering committee composed of the librarian, another adult staff member (such as a parent volunteer), and students, would outline staff roles. The group would examine the library's mission and needs, taking into account the school context and student interests, as they developed an academically sound and personally fulfilling niche in the library. Some of the possible roles that students assume include:

- Advisor: helping detemine policies and directions for library service
- Reviewer: for books, tapes, software
- Programmer: planning and implementing library events and services
- Communicator: making displays and posters, designing flyers and newsletters, presenting skits and public service announcements, "selling" the library, acting as a liaison to student government
- Producer: desktop publishing, videos, slide shows, transparencies, displays, Web pages
- Technician: operating, maintaining, troubleshooting, training others in educational technology
- Office assistant: processing, doing reception work, managing the circulation desk, filing
- Fund-raiser.

Together, students and staff can develop a job description for library student staff. A sample one follows (Pray 2.13):

Job Description for Library Aide

Functions of library aides:

- To help maintain the library in efficient work order.
- To acquire specialized skills and knowledge relating to various library procedures.

Duties: Most library aides will be assigned one or more of the following tasks:

- Working at the charge/circulation desk
- Shelving books
- Reading shelves
- Updating and filing magazines
- Creating displays and bulletin boards
- Assisting with special projects

Procedures:

- All library aides are to report on time as scheduled.
- Assignments will be given at the time of reporting.
- General school behavior rules are to be followed in the library.
- Library aides are expected to be courteous and helpful to other students at all times.

I have read and understand this job description. I agree to accept the privileges and responsibilities as described. I also understand that if I do not perform satisfactorily I give up the privilege of working in the library.

_____   _____
Student's signature   Parent/Guardian's signature

_____   _____
Date   Date

**CESAR CHAVEZ HIGH SCHOOL
8501 HOWARD DRIVE
HOUSTON, TX 77017**

Specific Tasks for Student Library Staff

What are possible student tasks? With sufficient training and appropriate supervision, students are capable of accomplishing myriad tasks. In fact, the limiting factor may be the librarian who either thinks there's not enough time to train students or who feels uncomfortable about delegating work to young people. However, seemingly minor tasks can be important to youngsters— and provide significant help to the library; turning on computers, collecting passes, delivering mail or equipment, putting up signs, and straightening the room are everyday tasks that take time and contribute to the overall well-being; of the library. The second section of this book offers training ideas for most of these tasks:

- Maintaining the facility: opening and closing, keeping the library tidy
- Circulation: check-out/in, doing overdue notices; inventorying
- Filing and shelving
- Processing materials: typing, covering, stamping, repairing, withdrawing
- Installing and registering computer software
- Operating, maintaining, and troubleshooting equipment
- Locating sources—and helping others to locate material
- Assisting in reading encouragement through storytelling, reviewing, tutoring, making displays and bookmarks
- Helping with programs and events: announcing, selling, hosting, seating

Using the steering committee approach, all library staff, including aides and volunteers, can sit down and brainstorm *all* of the potential tasks in the school library. In this way, students get to know the variety of possible functions in the library and to help determine their contribution to its overall operation. The librarian should prioritize each task so everyone understands what needs to be done first (such as circulation and shelving). As specific tasks are assigned, students should have the opportunity to volunteer first since their time and skills may be the most limited—and because their interest most influences their actions. Particularly with students, although the librarian should be sensitive to the wishes of all library staff, interests and capabilities probably constitute the main factors in task assignment. An easy method is to provide potential library student staff members with a checklist of possible tasks. They can then rank those jobs by preference. One good approach is to develop a core of responsibilities and functions expected of all library student staff, and tooffer a range of specialties for individual student staff.

Assessing Skills

One issue in making good use of library student staff is how to match student skills and library needs; while some tasks demand prerequisite skills (such as designing Web pages), other tasks can be learned with a minimum of training (such as checking out books). Assessing present and potential capabilities is an essential part of making good use of student, as well as adult, help. Particularly because school librarians are educators, they need to provide learning opportunities so students can be exposed to new skills and practice them.

A simple approach is to give students a checklist of skills used in performing duties in the library; students mark those skills they have, which they would like to learn, and which they want to avoid. The skills are then matched with the specific library task. Such a checklist might look like this:

- ☐ filing
- ☐ answering telephones
- ☐ typing
- ☐ word processing
- ☐ organizing
- ☐ writing
- ☐ reviewing
- ☐ illustrating
- ☐ lettering
- ☐ videotaping
- ☐ photographing
- ☐ mechanical work (carpentry, machine maintenance, lifting)
- ☐ fine motor skills (folding, stamping)
- ☐ cleaning
- ☐ researching
- ☐ teaching
- ☐ tutoring
- ☐ speaking
- ☐ reading aloud
- ☐ computer installing
- ☐ computer programming

As the librarian interviews students individually about their present skills and goals in their library work, she or he can negotiate with them for the best placement.

In some cases, a pre-test offers insight into student abilities. Students sometimes do not assess themselves accurately—or tend to give the answer that they think the librarian wants to hear rather than honestly say they don't know how to do a task. The following simple tests help diagnose student ability in a number of areas. Often a simulation of the task to be done is the most effective and authentic way to see how a student performs. It guards against any possible disruptions to ongoing library operations, yet helps the student decide realistically whether that task would be one that they would like to learn and do. For each test, the librarian should tell the students that their accuracy, speed, and thoroughness will be evaluated.

- Alphabetization: Have students put a cart of fiction books in alphabetical order by author's last name.
- Numerical order: Have students put a cart of non-fiction books in order by call number.
- Typing: Have students type file labels.
- Word processing: Have students create a sign using a computer.
- Writing: Have students compose a thank-you letter.
- Repairing: Have students repair a book or magazine.
- Artistry: Have students show examples of their work; have them make a bulletin board.

- Reviewing: Have students show a recent book report or have them write one on a new book.
- Reading: Have students follow written directions to do a multi-step task.
- Speaking: Have students give a 30-second announcement about a library event.
- Reading aloud: Have student read an excerpt of their own choosing.
- Teaching: Have students demonstrate how to use a library catalog, index, Internet, or CD-ROM.

These tests also serve as a diagnostic tool for training; thus, poor performance is all right; it just tells at which point the training should start. Students can then begin at a comfortable stage, and learn incrementally rather than feel overwhelmed and frustrated from day one.

Another possible way to assess skills—and the student's potential—is to ask for letters of reference and other evidence, such as prior student work and transcripts. These documents are actually good practice for students as they explore the world of work. Putting together a portfolio of desktop publishing samples or soliciting recommendations puts the responsibility of demonstrating existing expertise where it belongs and where the student has the most control: on her or his own shoulders.

Assessing personal skills

In most cases, technical skills can be taught. Interpersonal skills are more difficult to assess and to develop. Some student staff tasks require less human interaction than others, such as typing and discarding, but every student needs to develop a respectful relationship with other staff members. Basically, student staff should display the following traits:

☐ promptness
☐ ability to follow directions
☐ thoroughness
☐ follow-through
☐ ability to accept criticism
☐ flexibility
☐ enthusiasm
☐ patience
☐ trustworthiness
☐ dependability
☐ openness
☐ respectfulness
☐ helpfulness

Obviously, the best way to match students' personalities to library work is to know them personally and see them in action, both in the library and outside that environment. The librarian can observe how specific students get along with peers as well as adults and can check to see how they work independently. In short, the librarian would do well to get to know all the library users because some of them will likely be library staff candidates.

The next best approach is to interview the student applicants. As the conversation proceeds, the librarian should engage students on a personal level, letting them talk about themselves as real individuals. Is the student relaxed and open? Does she or he seem honest and enthusiastic? The librarian can also ask other school staff about the student in question, but sometimes student behavior and achievement can vary from class to class or change over time.

Regardless of the specific role, though, the librarian needs to clarify expectations, provide adequate training and supervision, and set reasonable standards.

Recruitment and Retention of
Student Library Staff

"How do I become a library aide?" one student asks.
"I don't know," replies another student. "But I *do* know that they can't keep anyone long. Must be a dumb place to work."

The library's mission may be exciting, its program great, and the adult staff wonderful. The librarian may believe in library student staff and have a full list of tasks for them to do. However, without effective recruitment and wise retention practices, student staff will be nil. On the other hand, a happy and well-trained student staff brings good business to the library—and good service.

Recruitment
In the final analysis, the best recruitment is through word-of-mouth by satisfied, existing library student staff. If they had a good experience, they will tell their friends. Especially if the librarian was pleased with their work, then chances are good that the new recruits and librarian will enjoy a pleasant relationship as well. Likewise, if the rest of the school faculty hear good news about library student staff, they will also pass on the word to prospective students come scheduling time.

However, if student staffing is a new venture, or if past experiences have been less than wonderful, then powerful recruitment is in order. The key is to motivate students by appealing to their needs for:
- Gaining recognition and status,
- Having a sense of belonging,
- Feeling useful and needed,
- Helping others,
- Developing new skills, amd
- Avoiding boredom.

Here are some concrete ways to get the word out about joining the library staff:
- Advertise throughout the building, with snappy soundbites:
  "Want to be in the driver's seat on the information highway? Sign up as a library aide!"
  "Join Information Central as a library student assistant!"
  "Help others surf the Net; become a library Net Navigator!"
  "Explore new worlds of information: join the Library Club!"
  "Make the library a better place: be a part of it—as a Library Team member!"
  "Wanted: YOU! for the library student staff!"
  "Get on the inside track; become a library intern!"
- Use colorful paper and well-designed graphics to attract attention and show how special the library is. Produce an upbeat rap for a public announcement.

- Get to know school counselors and advisors. Talk with them about the kind of student staff needed in the library. Provide them with the library checklist of tasks and skills so they can use it when scheduling students or suggesting co-curricular activities to students.
- Get articles about the library written in school publications, such as the student newspaper, yearbook, or parent newsletter. By profiling student library staff, these communication channels let others know about staffing possibilities and achievements.
- Photograph library student staff, and show them off in the library and other display areas in the school. Post *Student Staff of the Month* photos both to recognize outstanding work as well as to recruit those students' friends.
- Talk to student groups, club advisors, parent meetings. Tell them about the benefits of working in the library. Show how library internships prepare students for college (mindful that research skills need to be incorporated in student staff training).
- Ask regular library student users. If they're already used to the place and select it freely, they may be good candidates for staff help.

Any method used to recruit students should include how to contact the librarian, a time frame for joining (some libraries start staff throughout the year while others have "windows of opportunity"), and the process for applying. An application form shows that the job merits serious consideration. It can be as easy as this:

- Name, grade, and homeroom
- Time available
- Reasons for applying
- Current skills
- Personal interests
- Expectations
- References

Such an application provides the basis for the next step: interviewing.

Interviewing Potential Student Library Staff

The first encounter with a new library student staff member is the most important, for it establishes the relationship between the two persons. Morever, it paves the way for effective library utilization of students.

The first encounter should include the basics: the library's mission, an overview of the functions within the library, the role of library student staff, the role of the other staff and their relationship to the student, and the specific contributions and goals of the individual student. The librarian needs to set forth the basic expectations of the student—and the student's expectations of the library staff. The librarian should use the student's application as the foundation for the interview, and should build upon the student's strengths.

Since this first encounter sets the tone for further interaction, it should include some personal sharing. It is helpful if the librarian can find a mutual interest or value, such as love of reading or school dedication. The librarian might share some personal information, such as a mutual hobby or family background or music preference. Students need to see the librarian first as a person, someone whom they can trust and respect. Until that link is established, the librarian will be be considered as an impersonal "Them."

By the time the interview is finished, the student should have some idea of direction, some rapport with the librarian, and a feeling of anticipation for starting as a staff member. The librarian should have an idea of the student's capabilities and interests, time commitment, and how the student interacts with others.

In some cases, the librarian may end the interview by drawing up a written contract between the library and student; such documentation can lay a concrete foundation for future relationships. Furthermore, it provides a model for future work experiences. In any case, expectations should be clarified from the start. A rubric for behavior, including competencies, should be given and explained at the first meeting or application time. An example follows. If the student does not agree with the standards then he or she will probably not be comfortable helping in the library. It is much easier for the student to self-select out of the program at the beginning and not lose face or time than to get involved with a program that is unsuitable—and difficult to extricate from later on.

Great Expectations: Student Library Staff
What you, the student staff, can expect:
- Chances to learn more about the school and the library: information, reading, research, technology
- Chances to do a variety of activities or to specialize
- A individualized program to match your interests and skills
- Chances to explore the library science profession
- Chances to work with like-minded students and adults
- Personal help
- "Inside" privileges
- A chance to make a difference
- Fun—and occasional food!

Typical library activities:
- Circulation/main desk coverage
- Word processing and design
- Technical assistance
- Book and magazine processing
- Filing and shelving
- Videotaping
- Display and artwork
- Reviewing and writing

Librarian expectations of you, the student staff:
- Dependability
- On-task behavior
- Willingness
- Courtesy and respect to all library users and staff
- Ability to learn the job and ask for help when you need it
- Self-direction when a skill is mastered

Student staff expectations of adult library staff:
- Courtesy and respect
- Sufficient training and support so you can do your job
- Fair treatment and grading
- Opportunity for growth

Process:
- Match interests and needs
- Learn the skill
- Perform it independently
- Acfquire more skills

Our basic philosophy is that We're A Learning Community!

Orientation

An orientation to the library, describing its services, is essential, for it makes it easier for students to see their role within the total picture. This tour also gives the rest of the staff an opportunity to connect with the student and show their interest and support. A simple approach is for the librarian to physically tour the facility with the student and describe the tasks associated with each part of the library:
- Circulation desk: student check-out/in, generating overdue notices
- Magazine rack: checking in magazines and filing them
- Display area: creating attractive displays and signs for other students
- Pamphlet file: clipping and filing articles
- Computer stations: installing, inputting, troubleshooting, instructing, word processing, graphics
- Workroom: processing, repairing, withdrawing, producing.

During the tour the librarian should be sensitive to student responses. Do the students' eyes light up when they see the posters file? Do they get excited about seeing new books? Do they say they actually *like* typing? Do their fingers itch to get onto the computer? Those behaviors signal potential tasks that will both carry out the library's mission and intrigue and excite the student.

Sometimes the student comes in with very little knowledge or expertise about the library. The tour may trigger an interest. It is important to convey the message that library work is an ongoing learning experience, that students can and should grow on the job. Students also need to feel assured that someone will show them how to do a task, and that a learning curve is expected.

On the professional end, the librarian needs to look at the student's attitude: the willingness to learn and to help. Perhaps a student has never worked in a library before; it may be easier to teach that person than to put up with a student who thinks he or she is an expert but contributes little to the library and would rather show off skills that are counter productive, such as knowing how to crash a computer system.

By workingwith students' own interests based either on strengths or areas that they want to pursue, the librarian can take advantage of natural tendencies and focus on building both student *and* library niches.

Supervision

Supervision can make or break the effective use of student staff. A delicate balance exists between breathing down a student's neck and abandoning him or her. Unfortunately, each student has a different response to supervision, so the librarian needs to be sensitive to each student's needs and comfort zone. Fortunately, assuring a safe and positive learning environment provides a solid foundation for all supervision. Some of the features for such a grounding include:

- Staff awareness of their own behavior and the behaviors of students
- An atmosphere that encourages expressing genuine feelings
- Openness to discovering and recognizing alternatives
- A spirit of learning
- Social contracts—agreed-upon rules that are implemented and enforced
- Stress management (Curwin 34-42)

Supervision, by the way, does not have to done by the librarian alone. Paraprofessionals, parent volunteers, even student expert, can supervise staff. The critical factors are the supervisor's knowledge—and the presence of an adult somewhere in the library. (Each state has regulations concerning adequate classroom and library supervision.)

The intensity of supervision is typically correlated with the student's ability and dependability. As the student is learning a new skill, close supervision is necessary, not only to ensure that the job will be done correctly, but also because the librarian or supervisor needs to be available to answer students' questions and clarify details about the particular function. As the student demonstrates competency and trustworthiness, then supervision can assume a lighter touch.

Students recognize degrees of supervision, and value autonomy because of the trust that it implies. Students also realize when they are reined in that it may be because they have abused their role or have slipped in their quality of work. Most take the hint and improve, especially if the supervisor explains the reason for the tightened controls.

Sometimes supervision has a negative connotation. That doesn't have to be the case. Probably the most most positive situation is when the supervisor and the student work side by side. The task doesn't have to be the same; the important factor is the interaction between the two people. If the work allows for conversation, casual talk about school and personal interests can strengthen the bond between supervisor and student. Having a supervisor nearby can also comfort the student: Someone is around if the going gets rough. In general, if supervision is considered a safety net for the student, issues about "lurking" won't arise.

Social Interaction

One of the main motivations and reinforcements for effective student staff is social interaction. Hopefully, library student staff work because it's fun, as much as because it's a worthwhile endeavor. That friendly and positive spirit rubs off onto the users and makes the library a more pleasant place to work.

The most obvious social interaction is between peers. Students who work at the same time may do projects together. The librarian can set up these assignments as a way for student staff to bond and help each other. This mutual support can lead to peer instruction in library tasks, and can facilitate large-scale library activities such as a book fair or inventory. This kind of collaboration requires careful observation by the librarian or other supervisor, since productivity needs to remain at a high quality.

Sometimes when three or more student staff members who are friends prior to working in the library do a task together, they form a cohesive group that can challenge the authority of the supervisor. (This tends to happen in high school situations.) The counterproductive group dynamic can become very strong, and the supervisor then needs to separate the students and their tasks, or appeal to a higher mutual goal.

However, the usual picture, especially in middle grades, is a group of like-minded students who work together for the benefit of the library and the enjoyment of the group itself. Such a feeling occurs in library clubs and other social-based library groups, and can be reinforced by the librarian through special privileges (e.g., free copier privileges, no fines, use of telephone for emergencies) and occasional celebrations such as year-end parties and gift exchanges.

Good friendships can also be developed between librarian and staff as adults assume mentor relationships. Once a trusting relationship is built between the two, then honest talk can occur, and both parties can benefit from straightforward observation. The student may feel freer to talk about grumblings of peers—and the librarian can accept the criticism more gracefully. Likewise, the librarian can pass on information to a trusted student staff member who can relay it to peers in a non-threatening manner. Beyond the day-to-day concerns of the library, the positive and respectful personal relationship between adult and student staff provides a safe haven for youth—and a model that they can rely on in difficult times. The only caution is that the adult remain in control and not jeopardize his or her integrity or responsibility by becoming too friendly or imprudent.

Recognitions

Everyone likes to be recognized for work well done. Young people who are still forming their self-image especially appreciate having a respected adult take note of their efforts. A smile and a simple word of thanks for that extra push can brighten a student's day. Rewards and reinforcements are necessary elements of a good student staff program. While intrinsic motivations is a goal for effective staff management, students appreciate concrete signs of worthiness. Here are suggestions for practical and fun ways to show students that the staff cares:

- Certificate of thanks
- Library pin
- Letter of recommendation
- Nomination for school or local recognition
- Photo as student staff of the week or month
- Gift book
- A day off to do other schoolwork

- First chance to do desirable jobs (e.g., handling the desk, delivering mail, whatever is the "hot" task)
- Opportunity to make policy decisions
- Free copying privileges for the period
- Praise
- Party
- Food!

Disciplinary Actions

You can't please all of the people all of the time. What do you do when a student staff doesn't work out? Obviously, the librarian wants to facilitate increased student productivity and potential—or to find a better match for their capabilities. Setting up an environment for success is the best preventive measure against discipline problems. Here are some of those environmental factors:

Expectations: Are they in written form? Are they clear? Are they fair? Are they developed jointly by the librarian and the entire staff, both adult and student? Are expectations enforced consistently? Are there fair consequences for noncompliance?

Training: Does the student have the prerequisite skills to learn the task (e.g., alphabetization, sequencing, typing)? Is it clear? Is it thorough? Does it cover most of the probable situations? Does the student understand it? Bottom line: Can the student do it?

Communication: Is it mutually respectful? Is it based on trust, openness, and honesty? Is it fair and objective? Is it confidential when appropriate? Do both parties understand it? Is feedback immediate and accurate?

Some general principles are useful when taking action when misbehavior occurs. Curwin offers eight suggestions:
- Implement consequences consistently.
- State the rule and consequence.
- Be close to the student when implementing the consequence.
- Use direct eye contact with the student in question.
- Use a soft, yet firm, objective voice.
- Catch students being good.
- Correct students in private.
- Accept no excuses, bargains, or whines. (Curwin 95-98)

What are some of the specific problems that may occur when working with library staff? Here are representative scenarios and possible reasons for them:

Sloppy work: Misfiled books or cards; misspellings; gaps in work or sequence; poor handwriting.
Possible causes: lack of training, lack of understanding, lack of resources, lack of time, physical disabilities, distraction (either physical or emotional), conflicting attitude.

Low productivity: Little work done; work redone several times; wrong task done.
Possible causes: lack of training, lack of understanding, lack of resources, physical disabilities, distraction (either physical or emotional), conflicting attitude, perfectionism.

Inconsistence: Of attendance, productivity, attitude.
Possible causes: distraction (either physical or emotional), conflicting priorities, stress.

Disrespect: Of people (users, staff), equipment, materials, facilities.
Possible causes: lack of self-esteem, unawareness of own actions, lack of training, conflicting attitude.

Note that distractions can arise from a number of factors: noise, friends, physical discomfort, personal problems or concerns, medication, illness, substance abuse. Some of these are under the student's control; others are less so. Moreoever, some distractions are situational (such as a fire drill or anxiety about a test the following period) while others are ongoing or long-term (such as asthma or an abusive parent).

Behavioral problems can arise from student immaturity. The clown, the whiner, the "brat" occasionally act out, sometimes to the librarian's discomfort or annoyance. These students usually are looking for a way to belong and to feel important—and aren't going at it in a constructive way. Usually, natural consequences take care of the problem (if the student gets testy, peers avoid him or her). Doing the unexpected is a way to break the pattern, for example, walking away from a power struggle. In the long run, librarian acceptance and encouragement is the best policy. Here is a list of misguided behavior goals, and ways that the librarian can deal with them on an immediate basis:

Attention
Behaviors: clowning, playing tricks, being forgetful or negligent
Adult responses: ignore, redirect behavior, give choice

Power
Behaviors: aggression, defiance, disobedience, hostility, stubbornness, resistance
Adult responses: withdraw from power struggle, let both parties cool off, problem-solve later

Revenge
Behaviors: rudeness, violence, destructiveness, retaliation
Adult responses: withdraw from cycle, let both parties cool off, problem-solve later, win student over

Feelings of inadequacy
Behaviors: passive, quits, avoids trying, escapes through drugs
Adult responses: train for success through small steps, be patient, don't pity.
Excitement, Peer acceptance, Superiority (usually in teens)
Behaviors: risky behavior, avoidance of routine, ingratiation or put-downs
Adult responses: explain safety factors, redirect to positive results (Nelsen, 64; Dinkmeyer, 19).

However, in the final analysis, students are responsible for their own actions. The librarian's role is to help students to know and accomplish their responsibilities. When conflicts occur, then a problem-solving mode should come into play.

In some cases, the problem needs to be accepted as the librarian's. She or he might be uncomfortable with a student's visible ringed belly button or pink Mohawk. However, if the student does the work, the librarian has no real complaint (as long as the student is within the school's dress code). The librarian may express personal feelings about the dress, but should probably try to ignore the student's appearance and concentrate on the job being done. Some students actually try to dress provocatively to point out that appearances are deceiving. Such was the case with one heavily tattooed and head-shaven honor student.

If, on the other hand, the problem negatively affects library services, then the librarian time needs to set aside time to deal constructively with the situation. Basic steps in that process include:

1. Understanding and clarifying the problem
The behavior or outcomes should be described objectively, and its impact stated so the student understands: "I have noticed that you misshelve at least half of the books. This makes it harder for other people to find them. Why are you misshelving them?" The goal should be to solve the problem, not to punish the student. The underlying reason for the problem may not be obvious. For instance, in misshelving the student may be dyslexic—or embarrassed in front of friends.

2. Brainstorm alternatives:
The reason helps determine the solution. For example, in the first case, either the student gets help in overcoming the physical disability or changes tasks; in the second case, the student either needs to feel more self-confident and reinforced about the task's importance or needs to change tasks. In any case, the student should come up with the alternatives first because it not only validates the student's opinion but also demonstrates that the librarian listens.

3. Evaluate the alternatives:
What are the consequences of each alternative? Both the student and the librarian can say what they like about the alternative and what they don't like about it. It is wisest to eliminate those solutions that either party cannot accept. To often the librarians alternative is to tell the student, "Just deal with it." Such a directive represents a closed attitude that does not bode well for future librarian-aide relationships.

4. Choose a solution:
Ideas can be changed or combined, but both parties should agree with the final decision.

5. Commit to the solution and determine a time to evaluate it.
A written contract emphasizes the importance of the solution; teenagers in particular sometimes need that formal agreement. The evaluation should also be negotiated at the time of commitment, so both parties will know in advance how changes will be observed and measured.

While the best approach is one-to-one, sometimes an outside adult needs to get into the picture. Most schools have a grievance procedure. The counselor is usually the first outside person involved in conflict resolution. Further steps are normally increasingly formal. However, in most cases, the problem remains local—which it should be.

In some cases, the best solution is to part company in a staff relationship. The healthiest scenario is for the student to choose that alternative rather than the librarian, for then it is the student who is in control and responsible for the decision. Remember, not every student is perfectly fitted to work in the library. Some librarians have the feeling that they have failed if they have not won over every student or made each one into exemplary library staff. As in the motto, "Teachers can only teach; it is the student who has to learn," so too the librarian cannot provide a niche for every student as a library staff member. Nonetheless, student and librarian can remain friends and can sustain the respective roles of librarian and library user. And, hopefully, the library has enough resources and services that it *can* make a meaningful connection in some way with each student along the academic path.

Training Student Library Staff

"Training? I don't have time for that on top of everything else!"
"Training! It's the heart of what I do!"

Which statement reflects your attitude and practice?
One main factor in effective utilizing library student staff is effectively training them. When students learn how to do a task well and contribute to the library through their service, they become positive ambassadors to the library and also improve their self-esteem. Thus, the time spent in explaining how to work in the library is a valuable investment. This chapter presents some of the underlying principles in training young people for library work.

The Learning Environment

Do you work with students one-on-one? Do you train student staff as a whole? Do you have a choice? Most classroom learning involves a constant review-new concept-practice-test cycle as groups of students acquire greater information and skills. In contrast, library student staff are usually few in number any one period, and most of their time is spent doing a long-term task. While a few libraries echo the academic model of constant learning, most librarians have student staff in order to carry out library service. As a result, librarians usually spend much less time teaching, although they may answer individual student questions and provide added depth in follow-up training throughout the year, depending on library and student needs.

One model of library student staff training is based on the idea of a library club or coordinated intern program. All library student staff meet regularly, say twice a month, where they receive training together. This approach allows the librarian to train a group at a time, thus increasing instructional productivity, with the assurance that everyone is getting the same information. What's more, students can learn from watching each other (although they may learn some *wrong* skills as well). The librarian gets to see the students practice the new skills over the next weeks, and build any issues that arise into the next meeting's agenda.

If the program is considered a social gathering as well, then a mix of training and fun can motivate students to attend regularly and build a sense of camaraderie. This model occurs more naturally in the middle or junior high school level than high school, partly because school structure typically provides more activity time, partly because students usually have fewer time commitments, and partly because a structured social group within the school is more appealing.

In a high-powered school setting, particularly where library student staff also manage computer systems, the intern program may modify the group training model. Knowing that the library and computer stations need to be up and running the first day of school, and that heavy-duty training may be difficult after the start (particularly if it's hard to find a joint meeting time), the librarian may give an intensive two- to three-day training before formal classes start—in the same way that fall sports practice sometimes predates school starting date. Students then upgrade their skills during the year through one-on-one training or monthly "mini-conferences."

In most cases, though, librarians train student staff on a one-on-one or small group basis, typically all the student staff who work during one school period. Training may be the same for all students, or it may vary according to period or student interest. The advantage of such an arrangement is that it fosters individualized instruction and student staff specialization. The disadvantage is obvious: the commitment of time. The amount of training time at any one point, and general scheduling of training, vary more in this approach. Typically, the librarian gives an overview of the job and trains for basic library operations such as circulation and shelving. Additional training depends on library need (such as inventory or overdues), student capability and interest, and available time. Librarians in this situation need to look at alternative teaching methods in order to maximize student learning—and contributing. Flexibility—and good documentation—are key factors for successful small-group and individual training.

General Learning and Training Concepts

Training library student staff differs from other classroom teaching because library work consists of specific skills. Even those courses that demand technical expertise, such as ceramics or computer programming, introduce those techniques to further student creativity. While some library skills lend themselve to student customization, such as posters and storytelling, most duties are, frankly, a matter of consistent and accurate application. Thus, most library staff instruction fits under the model of training rather than academic instruction.

What are the critical features that distinguish training from most classroom instruction?

- Focus on change
- Task-specific
- Short-term time frame
- Practical, results-based
- Immediate application
- Mastery level goal
- Usually experiential: students experience the task, examine its elements, learn the process, and apply it.

How do student characteristics influence training?

- Students need some direction, but less as they mature.
- Students have experience; most have used a library by the time they are in middle school.
- Students have a real life outside school, and appreciate training that helps them in that real world.
- Students like to interact.
- Students need repetition.
- Students have limited time; they have other classes and outside activities.

Even with the best intentions and thorough planning, training can fail because of a student's personal experiences with or feelings about training. Here are some factors that can interfere with student learning:

- Lack of prerequisite skills (e.g., the student doesn't know how to alphabetize so has difficulty learning how to shelf accurately)
- Different learning style (e.g., if all instruction is given orally, and the student learns best by reading, then the training will be less effective)
- Fear of criticism
- Negative past training. (If it's in library skills, then it will be harder for the present librarian to overcome past impressions. If the past negative was in a totally different subject, the degree of transferred negativity may be less.)
- Competing priorities (other courses, sports meets, personal problems or activities)
- Bad pacing
- Lack of significance: just because a task is important to the librarian doesn't mean it's important to the student.

What are the implications for training practices?
- Make it useful and meaningful.
- Make it hands-on.
- Deal with mixed abilities.
- Consider a variety of learning styles.
- Let students share experiences.
- Make it enjoyable!

Designing Training Sessions

If library training is going to work, it needs to be well prepared and executed. If the librarian trains in a convincing and engaging manner, students will respect the trainer and carry out the needed task with more conviction and efficiency. The overall design of training includes the initial decision, preparation, implementation, and follow-through. While most library training is small-scale, considered thinking and planning will pay off in higher student productivity.

Determine the objective of the training
- What library mission or goal is being addressed?
- Who will take the training?
- What are the desired student outcomes? What will they be able to do, under what conditions, and to what degree?

Design the training
- What do students already know? How can they be assessed?
- What learning styles need to be addressed: auditory, visual, kinesthetic?
- What is the time frame, both in terms of the specific training, and in terms of its introduction into the school year?
- Who will conduct the training: librarian, other paid staff, adult volunteers, student staff?
- What is the format: presentation/demonstration, fact sheet/manual, computer-based training, videotape, audiotape?
- What resources are needed: training aids, handouts, supplies?
- How will the training be evaluated? The goal is student performance!

Conduct the training
- Define the task and outcome.
- Have the students experience the task, at least by watching the trainer demonstrate it.
- Share experiences and reactions.
- Explain the process.
- Check for understanding.
- Have students practice applying the process.

Evaluate the training
- Content: level of difficulty, level of usefulness
- Delivery: format, pacing sequence, clarity, time frame
- Resources: handouts, aids, equipment
- Student performance.

Training Methods

Sometimes the best training is not a formal presentation by the librarian, but a demonstration by a student peer or a clear guide sheet that a student can use independently. Librarians should provide a variety of training methods in order to reach the wide variety of students that they supervise.

Methods of training depend on several factors: student ability, time frame, depth of knowledge desired, linkages with other learning, number and arrangement of students. Here are some possible delivery methods, including the relative advantages and disadvantages of each.

Presentations constitute the traditional way to provide information— and often are the least effective way to train stduents. Specific techniques include lecture, panel (to show different points of view), and introductory audiovisual shows. To engage students, presentations should include some type of visual aid or guiding sheet. Students should also have a chance to ask questions along the way, and try out the task under supervision. A presentation on lab use is typical.

Demonstrations model correct techniques or processes. The demonstration should be simple, and everyone should be able to see and hear it. Students should be engaged during the demonstration; one easy way is to check for understanding by asking questions. Students should be encouraged to ask their own questions in order to clarify procedures. To be effective, any demonstration should be immediately followed by an opportunity for students to practice those same skills and get specific feedback on their performance. Circulation procedures are often demonstrated, for instance.

Case studies provide realistic situations that require problem-solving. They encourage transfer of knowledge to specific, real-life application. Good case studies emphasize process as much as result, and thus should encourage multiple approaches or solutions. One disadvantage of case studies is that they often require much development time. Case studies would be a good method to teach ways to deal with difficult patrons.

Buddy coaching is time-intensive but effective for specific skills on a need-to-know basis, such as doing discards. It encourages partnership, so can be useful for developing student mentors. The librarian has to be sure that the trainer knows the task well, and that she or he can communicate it effectively. The librarian also has to make sure that the training is mainly coaching rather than mainly buddying.

Training Aids

Training aids can make learning much easier—for both the trainer and the trainee. Because they are usually visual, they help the visual learner in particular. They can usually be given to a student who prefers to learn independently. Aids can also provide a permanent record of the process, so staff can refer to them later when working on the job.

A few guidelines are applicable to all training aids.
- Aids should be clear and legible.
- Sequential information should be numbered or somehow marked to be followed step by step.
- Important features should be accentuated: by arrows, type differentiale, or color.
- Aids should be pilot-tested before they are used to train others.

The following list describes advantages and disadvantages of different training aids.

Transparencies allow a large group to see main points, both in text and in picture. Transparencies are easy to make and to use, but they need an overhead projector.

Charts present facts graphically. They can be used as posters for permanent reference. Charts should be simple, colorful, and clear.

Videotapes add motion to the training. In-house productions can show how a specific library does a specific task. Videotaping requires certain equipment—and competent crew to both tape and edit afterwards. Additionally, students need equipment to view the tape. Ideally, viewing can be done next to the site where the work is to be done.

Computer multimedia can be a very interactive aid, but development time is intensive unless a pre-packaged product is available (at a reasonable cost). Sometimes CD-ROMs and other software programs come with their own multimedia tutorials; these "tours" offer a way for students to learn at their own pace independently. One of the disadvantages of self-guided tours is that students may stray off-course and not learn from the experience. A quick check for understanding after the student is done makes it obvious whether the training was effective or not.

Dealing with Students Who Have Special Needs

Beyond the typical differences among students in terms of learning style and personality, some factors such as physical disabilities and major cultural differences require extra attention, sensitivity, and patience. In general, the librarian should assess each student in terms of prior knowledge and experience and present level of functioning.

As special students are being mainstreamed, the librarian should be particularly mindful to provide inclusive activities. As a rule of thumb, each training session should incorporate several senses: a handout, oral discussion, physical manipulation of equipment or supplies being explained. Likewise, time scheduling and group arrangement should be flexible to meet individual needs and allow for students to learn from each other. Some learning disabled students need extra-tight structure; some hard-of-hearing or visually limited need to be physically closer to the trainer; some physically challenged need a modified keyboard or extra space. By consulting with the resource specialist, the librarian can make those necessary accommodations while providing all students the opportunity for social interaction and acceptance.

Other students with special needs are those with multicultural heritages, especially those new to the United States. The librarian should get to know the student's cultural background and personal interests so they can be woven into training sessions. Training should incorporate visual clues so students can overcome possible language barriers.

On a more basic level, the librarian needs to provide a safe and accepting learning atmosphere so students can feel comfortable communicating and taking other learning risks. Regardless of the student's background or capability, each one has a contribution to make—and a need to belong and succeed.

Training Records

Particularly if a number of people train a number of student staff, it becomes difficult to maintain an accurate record of student progress. Probably the easiest way to keep track of training is to develop a training spreadsheet with the skill on one axis and the student's name on the other axis. The cells can be coded as follows:

- / means the concept was introduced.
- X (is added to the /) means the student practiced the concept.
- ■ means the student mastered the concept.

Thus, a sample record might look like this:

	Shelve	Check out items	Make signs
Sasha C.	/	X	
Mario F.	■	/	X
Kim L.	X	■	X

Students can monitor their own progress, with the librarian making occasional spot checks. This method offers additional benefits: Students assume responsibility for their own learning, adult staff can use the tracking system to assign students tasks throughout the year, directions for training can be easily determined, and assessment can be facilitated.

Evaluation

Evaluation is a critical, and often overlooked, function in training student staff. Typically, evaluation is done operationally, if the student can do the task, then the training was effective. However, more formal assessment tools can be introduced to make training more effective.

A simple formative assessment that is easily incorporated is checking for understanding by asking students questions during training: "What would you do if...?" "Jose, explain that last step to Jackson."

As students are first practicing a task, the librarian can give immediate and specific feedback. Any statements should be clear and accurate, and descriptive rather than judgmental. Likewise, students should be able to give the trainer ongoing feedback.

Summative evaluation may be used to evaluate specific training, procedures themselves, and overall library experience. Here are some approaches:

- Analyze videotaped training or practice.
- Observe practice and discuss it afterwards.
- Rate training effectiveness along specific lines, such as content, pacing, clarity, aids.
- Give one positive comment about the training and one idea on how to improve it.

Not only should individual evaluations be analyzed, but the overall quality of evaluation should be examined for trends. If, for example, student performance is poor across the board, then the training process probably needs overhauling. If one function is not being carried out, then either training is inadequate or expectations may be unrealistic.

When grading students for their extended period of work, a compilation of assessments is needed. The goal is to examine the student's overall consistent (or inconsistent) performance. The following form, designed by Donna Dalton, provides an easy way to categorize and enumerate student work. The guidelines should be given to student staff at the beginning of the grading period so expectations will be clear, and students can assess their own progress regularly.

Student Media Assistant Evaluation

In each of the following categories you will receive points for your performance in the areas of instructional assignments, assisting students and teachers, as well as media office duties. These points will be totaled for a grade each nine weeks.

Reliability:
(5) Dependable
(4) Usually dependable
(3) Reliably follows directions
(2) Careless in following directions
(1) Unsatisfactory

Quality of Work:
(5) Outstanding
(4) Above average
(3) Average
(2) Poor
(1) Unsatisfactory

Initiative:
(5) Displays initiative to a high degree
(4) Sometimes goes ahead on own
(3) Performs regular duties only
(2) Weak in regular duties
(1) Unsatisfactory

Undesirable traits:
(-5) Has too many visitors
(-5) Absent often
(-5) Talks too much
(-5) Leaves work area without permission
(-5) Is loud and boisterous
(-5) Other _____

Attitude:
(5) Very enthusiastic
(4) Shows interest generally
(3) Shows interest in some areas
(2) Lacks interest in work
(1) Unsatisfactory

Cooperation:
(5) Very cooperative
(4) Usually cooperative
(3) Helps only when requested
(2) Doesn't work well with others
(1) Unsatisfactory

Punctuality and Attendance:
(5) Excellent
(4) Very good
(3) Good
(2) Poor
(1) Unsatisfactory

Grading system:
25-30 points.........A
19-24 points.........B
14-18 points.........C
9-13 points...........D
8-below points......F

Notes

Chapter 2

Skills and Concepts of Student Library Staff

This section of the book provides outlines for training sessions. Each one includes activity description, objectives, process, demonstration ideas, student activities, follow-up, and evaluation. Training is grouped into seven major library functions or services, with an introductory page delineating the critical features of the common characteristics for the group of tasks.

Training library student staff differs from most classroom instruction in several ways: number of students, grouping arrangement, length of time, instructional designate, and outcomes. While is it possible that the librarian would teach students simultaneously for a full class period, presenting principles and providing practice time, that scenario is the exception rather than the rule. Particularly since the librarian often juggles staff training in the midst of classroom visits, training needs to be specific and quickly applied. Thus, single-concept task training is the norm. Additionally, guide sheets and reference pages are typical training devices, the concept being that after using these aids, the student can perform the needed task and will ask the librarian only specific, clarifying questions.

With these caveats noted, the following framework provides a full look at potential training sessions.

Function description:	Brief heading describing the subject to be learned.
Objectives	A list of instructional learning objectives related to the function.
Process	The main concepts and steps to consider when training student to perform the function.
Demonstration ideas	Tips to guide the trainer to facilitate student learning; sample training aids may be provided.
Student activities	Specific steps that students carry out independently or under initial supervision; sample guide sheets may be provided.
Follow-up	Next steps in enriching or expanding the function or training.

Evaluation   Guidelines for assessing student performance and training experience; as much as possible, the criteria for evaluation should be given at the beginning of the activity. In the final analysis, if the student can independently perform the function competently, the training is successful.

Orientation

At the first meeting, students should know the library's mission and their role within that context. Students should be given a job description, a set of expectations for the job, and, optionally, a library contract to assure that both parties agree upon the student staff's role.

Students should also have an idea about the library's working environment. The librarian should introduce the student to the other staff members, both student and adult, and to library volunteers. This is the time that the librarian can show the student where to store personal property such as school bags during work, how to check in, and procedures for leaving during the period. Informally, the librarian can talk about the general atmosphere of the library and how staff interact.

Because the student needs to feel comfortable in her or his new working "home," a guided tour of the facility is imperative before other training begins. Students often are surprised to see the "other side" of the library that they have used in the past as a student patron. They love to see the behind-the-scenes nooks and crannies; they have just entered the inner circle!

At this point, safety and emergency issues should be discussed. Students should know safe practices and what to do in case of an emergency. In most instances, students have already been given instruction in emergency preparedess by classroom teachers. The librarian needs only to point out the unique characteristics of the library's situation.

The task of orienting the student can be shared by several people: the librarian, other paid staff, adult volunteers, and existing student staff. Whoever does the job, however, should be an expert and give an accurate, objective description of the library. Orientation sets the tone for future student relations, so great care is needed in order to provide a solid and positive foundation for the new student staff.

The library's mission

Objectives

The student will identify the library's mission, and give examples of functions that carry out the library's mission.

Process

The trainer shares the mission statement and shows how the mission is implemented through library resources and services.

Demonstration ideas

- Post the mission statement in a highly visible place in the library.
- Have the student find the mission statement in the student handbook and explain how the library fits into the school.
- Print the mission statement on a piece of paper, and then cut it up jigsaw-puzzle style. Have the student, or group of students, put the pieces together and read the entire document aloud.
- After sharing the mission statement, pose possible functions and have the student decide which are aligned with the mission and which are not.

Student activities

Have students
- Express ways that you have seen the library carry out the mission.
- Share ideas on how you can help implement the library's mission.
- Make two columns: in the first column, write library functions that carry out the library's mission; in the second column, write potential library functions that would not be aligned with the library's mission.

Follow-up

Discuss the student's role within the context of achieving the mission. Show the library's facilities to the student, linking the orientation to the mission.

Evaluation

Can the student
- Explain the library's mission to a peer?
- Offer ways to help carry out the mission as a staff member?
- Point out the critical features of the mission, and suggest functions that would fall outside the mission?

Sample Library Mission Statement
The school library media center is an integral part of the school. Working within the context of the school's goals, the mission of the school library media program is to:

- Insure that students and staff are effective users of ideas and information.
- Provide a wide range of resources and information that satisfy the educational needs and interests of students.
- Provide a setting conducive to formal and informal learning.
- Provide access to information through cooperation with other resource centers.

Personnel and their roles

Objectives	The student will identify library personnel, describe their roles, and tell how the student's own role relates to other library staff.
Process	The trainer introduces the student to other library personnel, and describes their roles within the library as they relate to carrying out the library's mission. The trainer explains how the student staff member's role relates to the rest of the staff and to the library's mission.

Demonstration ideas

- Introduce the student to all library personnel, and have them explain their roles.
- Show the student the library's organization chart, preferably with pictures of all library personnel.
- Share the job description of each library staff member with the student, and have the student explain how the job relates to the library's mission.

Student activities

- Match each library staff person with each library function.
- Make a 3"x5" card for each library function you can think of.
- Place each card under the appropriate person on the organization chart.
- Draw a sociograph that visually shows how each library staff member relates to the other. (Draw a circle for each staff person, and label it. Draw thick lines between people who work closely together, and draw thin lines between people who have only a slight working connection.)

Follow-up

Discuss the student's working relationship with the rest of the library staff. Negotiate with the student on feasible tasks that the student wishes to undertake as a staff member. Explain to the student that each staff member is responsible for some function of the library, and that the student may ask them for expert advice relative to the task.

Evaluation

- Identify all library personnel and describe their roles?
- Relate her or his role to the rest of the staff?
- Match specific tasks with specific personnel?

Personnel Policy Template

The success of the school library media program depends ultimately on the quality and productivity of the personnel responsible for the program. A well-educated and highly motivated professional staff, adequately supported by technical and clerical staff, is critical to the endeavor.

The school library media center staff consists of:

- The library media teacher, whose name is:
- The library technician, whose name is:
- The library clerk, whose name is:
- Parent volunteers, whose names are:
- Student aides, whose names are:

The role of the library media teacher is to coordinate all library media and information services. The library media teacher is a faculty member, and may be part of the management team. The library media teacher has the following expertise:

- Library and information science: organization, administration, and management
- Education: teaching and learning theories, curriculum development
- Communications: interpersonal, media forms
- Technology: telecommunications, computer systems and services, media production, facility design

The role of the support staff is to perform mainly clerical and technical duties in order to free professional staff to work directly and closely with students and faculty. Support staff have a general knowledge of library media program activities and specific skills necessary to perform their duties.

The role of the library technician is to facilitate the use and maintenance of technology and media production.

The role of the library clerk is to carry out secretarial and basic business operations, such as word processing, duplicating, filing, sorting, organizing, and keeping records.

The role of parent volunteers is to provide services that supplement the work of the regular staff.

The role of student aides is to assist in carrying out the library's mission.

Tour of the library facility

Objectives: The student will identify different parts of the library facility and explain what functions are carried out in each part.

Process: The student walks through the library. Each section is described in terms of the available resources and associated functions.

Demonstration ideas:
- Provide students with maps of the library, and have them match resources or functions with each particular area.
- Produce a video walking tour.
- Produce an audiocassette tape tour of the library, marking each section ahead of time so the student can identify the area.

Student activities: Have the student
- Use a map of the library and write relevant functions for each area.
- Match a list of resources to a list of areas within the library.
- On a list of questions, state where in the library those questions could be answered.

Follow-up: Determine what part of the library facility interests the student, and match that area to the related function (e.g., clipping file, display area, CD-ROM station).

Evaluation: Given a directional question, can the student point out the appropriate area?
Given a function, can the student link it to a specific part of the library?
Shown a map of the facility, can the student identify the kinds of resources or functions associated with the section?

Library Scavenger Hunt

Directions: Different parts of the library are labelled with an alphabet letter. Write down the letter that corresponds to the numbered function (listed below) that you can do in the library.

1. Find the call number of a book.
2. Find an atlas
3. Read a current magazine.
4. Make a photocopy.
5. Read a back issue of the school newspaper.
6. Find a pamphlet on AIDS.
7. Find a list of articles on a social issue.
8. Word process a report.
9. Find a dictionary.
10. Find an encyclopedia.
11. Use a CD-ROM magazine index.
12. Locate a fiction book.
13. Check out a book or magazine.
14. Find a recent local newspaper.
15. Find a two-month-old newspaper.
16. Read something on microfilm.
17. Find the computer rules.
18. Look at displays.
19. Find a book list.
20. Find out what books local libraries have.
21. Find out what magazines local libraries have.
22. Use the Internet.
23. Cut out magazine pictures.
24. Buy a book or magazine.
25. Ask for help.

Safety practices and emergency plans

Objectives: The student will follow safe practices and will know what to do in case of an emergency.

Process: Describe the safety issues associated with each function to be performed by the student, and demonstrate safe practices for each function. Share the library's emergency plans, and have the student practice what to do in case of an emergency. Explain legal issues that thestudent may have to encounter, such as harassment or property destruction; provide the student with ways to deal with these issues.

Demonstration ideas:
• Create learning stations for each area where the student needs to be aware of safety issues; have staff demonstrate safe practices.
• Create a safety sheet with diagrams so the student can follow correct procedures.
• Have the Red Cross give first aid instruction to the student.
• Have the student examine the library's first aid kit, giving suggestions on how to use each item.
• Show the emergency plan to the students, and walk through procedures with them.
• Give case studies about possible safety hazards or unsafe practices, and discuss appropriate action to take in each case.

Student activities:
• Have the student demonstrate safe and unsafe practices related to a specific function.
• Pose hypothetical situations to the students, and have them suggest or act out safe procedures for each scenario.
• Have the students brainstorm possible hazards and solutions on ways to deal with them.

Follow-up: Assign students specific tasks to do in case of emergencies, such as reporting to administration. Encourage the student to take first aid and CPR courses. Maintain a record of students with those skills.

Evaluation: Can the students
• Identify safety issues with the tasks they are assigned to, and demonstrate safe practices?
• Identify legal issues that they might encounter, and describe what action they must pursue to keep within the law?
• Explain what to do in case of an emergency?

Emergency Scenarios

1. An ice storm is approaching. Your job is to maintain the computers. You need to make sure that no data is lost and that the computers will stay in good working order. What do you do?

2. It's Monday morning and it's raining hard. As you enter the door, the librarian says, "Help me save the library; it's flooding!" What do you do?

3. Two boys are arguing, and they look like they're ready to fight it out in the library. What do you do?

4. You see a student cutting up a magazine that you just filed. What do you do?

5. A student threatens you. What do you do?

Basic Operations

All student staff need to know how to perform basic library operations: circulation, filing and shelving, notices, and inventory. These services are ongoing and necessary for the smooth working of the library. Students should feel comfortable filling in when any of these tasks need doing. For instance, if book carts are piling up, student staff should take it upon themselves to get those sources onto the shelves so students can use them. If a student is standing at the circulation desk, wanting to borrow a book, a free student staff member should rise to the occasion and check out the item so the student won't have to wait.

In fact, this kind of helping mindset needs to be emphasized before anything else. The spirit of service is the ultimate *modus operandi*. Since student staff represent the library, they need to be taught basic interpersonal skills, the kind that business receptionists employ. Some of the specifics include desk transactions, phone etiquette, and general interactions with library users and staff.

Next, students need to be familiar with library jargon, since it is used by staff and needs to be understood by library users. Trained student staff can act as translators for their peers when, for example, the librarian casually tells a student to look for the call number and the student staff member sees a blank look on the user's face.

Since a basic library service is the circulation of its resources, student staff should know how to make that happen. Part of that function is to treat the borrower in a friendly and courteous manner; presentation is as important as function.   Student staff also need to learn how to field questions at the desk since most of the school considers anyone behind the desk to be a library expert. An amazing number of questions are locational or basic, such as "Where is the pencil sharpener?" and "How can I find a fiction book?" Student staff can field such inquiries, thereby freeing the reference librarian to contend with sophisticated reference questions.

Students can use those resources that they can locate: in catalogs, in files, and on the shelves. Thus, a prime job of student staff is to file and shelve. While some knowledge of the Dewey Decimal Classification system is useful because it gives students a rationale for the arrangement of materials, attention to detail is actually more important because an out-of-sequence source or entry is essentially a lost item. Students need to appreciate the seriousness and minutiae of these tasks. Thus, the librarian needs to check student alphabetization and numerical skills, uphold high standards, and make sure that students can attain those high standards. Likewise, filing rules need to be rigorously followed.

Because materials need to be in constant circulation to maximize their use, timely overdue notices constitute a valuable service to the student body (and faculty) because they signal the worth of getting materials into the hands of the greatest possible number of users. Student staff assist in this process by making sure information is correct and that notices are efficiently distributed.

Finally, the library needs to know what materials it truly has on hand. Nothing is more frustrating and misleading to users than to look at a library catalog and think that a specific resource is available only to find a gap where the book or magazine should be. Therefore, an accurate inventory is needed to ascertain an accurate picture of library holdings. While it is disheartening to discover missing or lost volumes, it is worse not to know about those gaps. At least with knowledge, the librarian can replace those important volumes. The student staff's responsibility is to accurately report the staus of every resource.

Basic library etiquette

Objectives: The student will interact with the library public in an informed and courteous manner.

Process: The trainer discusses proper methods of dealing with the public, both face-to-face and over the phone. The trainer explains how library staff should interact. The trainer explains issues of socializing during working time. The trainer tells the student when to refer a question or situation, such as for donations or misbehavior.

Demonstration ideas:
- Role-play possible scenarios, such as welcoming people, answering the phone, and dealing with complaints, handling friends who want to chat.
- Demonstrate the proper volume, tone, and vocabulary to use when speaking with the public, with staff, and on the phone.
- Ask students what incidents they may have encountered when at a store or another library, and brainstorm how to handle interpersonal situations.
- Have different staff persons discuss personnel interactions.

Student activities: Have students
- Draw a flow chart diagramming steps to take in different situations.
- Practice using a "public" voice and vocabulary.
- Explain how they would react in various situations involving library etiquette.
- Act out appropriate and inappropriate ways to deal with the public and staff.

Follow-up: Explain some of the legal and safety issues that touch upon good public relations. In some cases, students may need training in assertive behavior (for those who don't want to say "no" to their friends).

Evaluation:

Given a scenario about dealing with the public, does the student offer an appropriate solution? Does the student

- have an audible, clear, and appropriate speaking manner?
- Refrain from socializing and gossiping?
- Demonstrate correct phone manners?
- Refer the public to the appropriate adult staff member at appropriate times?
- Remain respectful, calm, and objective under stressful situations?

Library Aide Proficiency Quiz (just for fun)

Name _____

           (First)   (Last)   (Alias)

Circle the Correct response.

1.   T   F   It is permissible to do wheelies with the book truck once all the books have been shelved.

2.   T   F   Is is allowable to use the dater to stamp the hands and forearms of the borrowers to call attention to the correct return date.

3.   T   F   The correct form of address for the librarian is "Hey, you!"

4.   T   F   The proper way to deliver library overdue notices is to fold them into paper airplanes and fly them to the appropriate teachers.

5.   T   F   "Bring this book back or we shall have to hurt you" is an acceptable way to personalize the overdue notices.

6.   T   F   Love notes found in return books may be posted on the library bulletin board.

7.   T   F   One of the benefits of being an assistant is a private lounge complete with soda dispenser and private phone.

8.   T   F   In hanging up library displays, it is allowable to climb the book shelves instead of a ladder.

9.   T   F   Student aides shall pay the librarian the minimum wage for the privilege of working in this fine facility.

10. T   F   This is a real quiz.

If you see the humor in this quiz, you will do quite nicely as a library aide.

It never pays to take ourselves too seriously, you know. (Pray 2.15)

Library terms

Objectives: The student will explain a variety of library terms.

Process: Point out that libraries have a specialized set of words to describe specific resources and functions. Define each word, and explain its use within the library's operations.

Demonstration ideas:
- Produce diagrams that point out different terms.
- Associate terms with related functions.
- Create a board game that quizzes students on library terms.

Student activities: Have the student
- Complete a library term crossword puzzle.
- Use library terms in sentences.
- Match definitions and terms.

Follow-up: Encourage students to keep a notebook of new library terms.

Evaluation: Given a term, can the student provide an accurate definition?
Can students associate terms with their applications?

Library Term Crossword

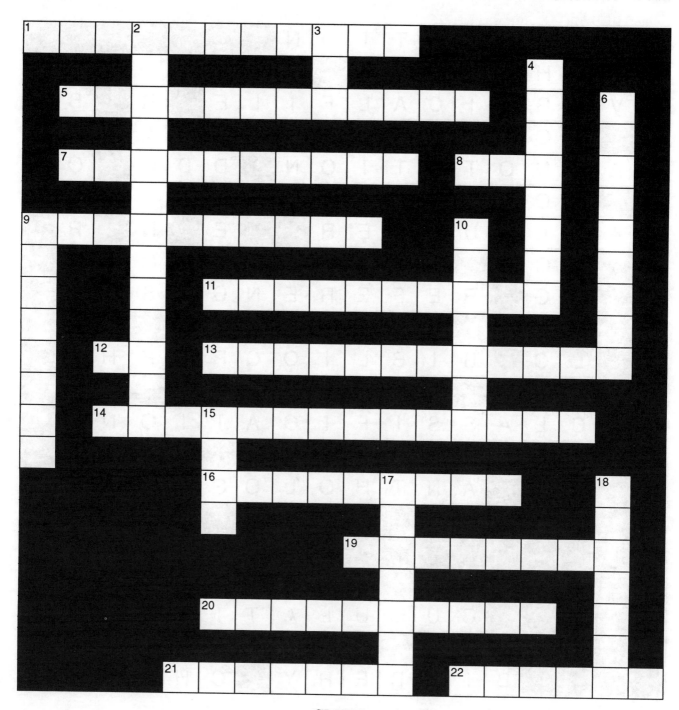

CLUES:

ACROSS
1 check-out and in of resources
5 file of clippings/pamphlets
7 brief description of work's content
8 Dewey Decimal Classification
9 number/author "address" of a work
11 detailed fact sources in library
12 Library of Congress
13 list of works
14 ordering of sources by subject
16 collection of works
19 summary of a text
20 several issues in one
21 firm that binds books/magazines
22 to record a loan

DOWN
2 in order by date
3 interlibrary loan
4 notations at end of catalog entry
6 information about a person's life
9 reference to a piece of information
10 selected passage from a text
15 book with a circulation problem
17 information center
18 list of library's collection

Library Term Crossword Answers

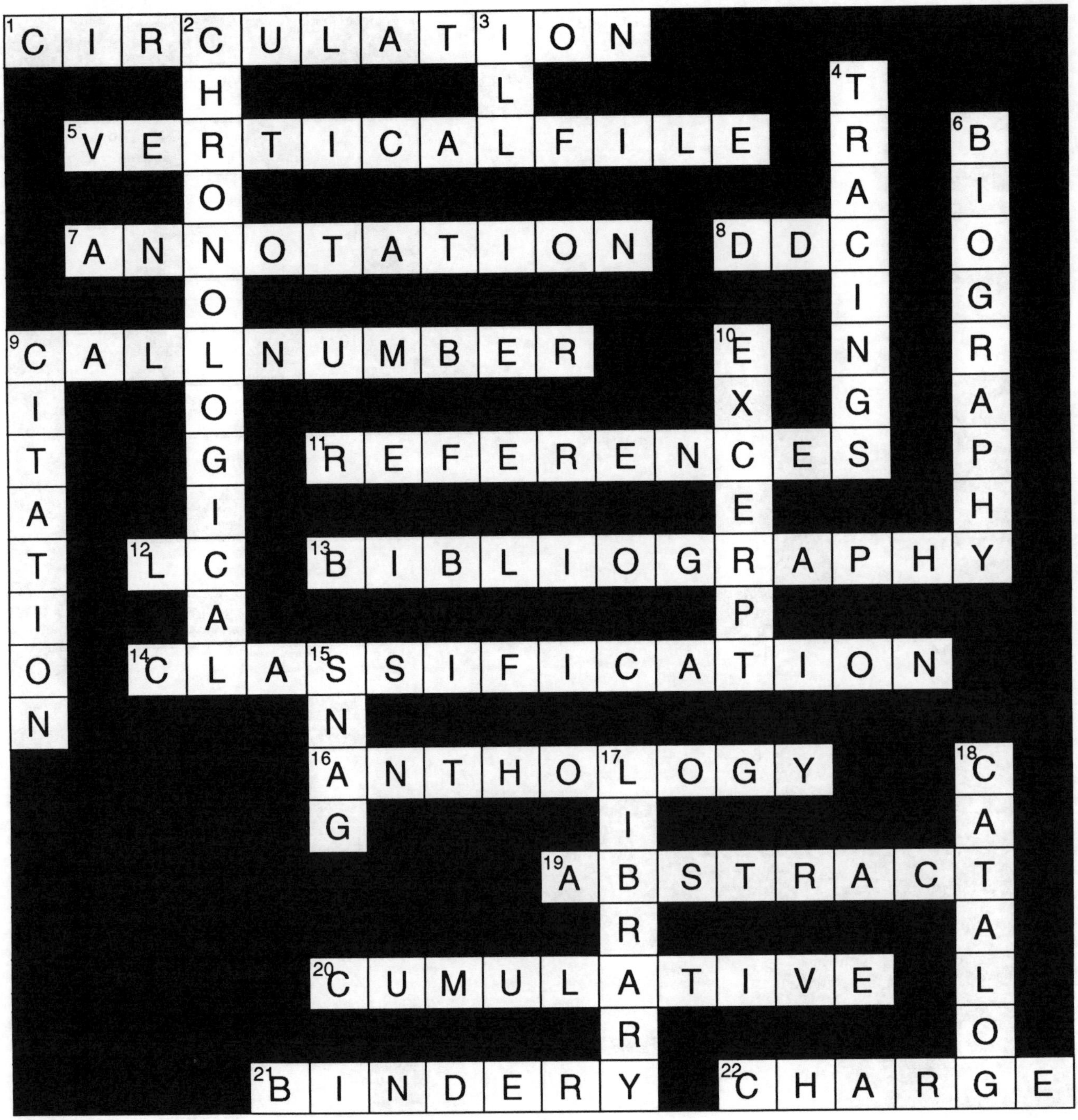

The completed crossword puzzle reads:

Across:
1. CIRCULATION
5. VERTICALFILE
7. ANNOTATION
8. DDC
9. CALLNUMBER
11. REFERENCES
12. LCA
13. BIBLIOGRAPHY
14. CLASSIFICATION
16. ANTHOLOGY
19. ABSTRACT
20. CUMULATIVE
21. BINDERY
22. CHARGE

Down:
2. CHRONOLOGICAL
3. ILL
4. TRACING
6. BIOGRAPHY
9. CITATION
10. EXCERP
15. SN
16. AG
17. LIBRARY
18. CATALOG

Check-out and check-in procedures

Objectives: The student will accurately check out and check in various library materials.

Process: The trainer demonstrates each step in checking out a book, a magazine, and other library materials. The trainer then demonstrates each step in checking in material. Exceptions to normal procedures should be highlighted afterwards.

Demonstration ideas:
1. Walk through the process once, verbally describing each specific step.
2. Next, have students walk through the process, saying aloud each step. Verbally coach student as they requested.
3. Next, have students walk through the process without comment. Give any suggestions afterwards.
4. Finally, have students do the process with a library user: the real thing. Critique the transaction afterwards.
5. Have students take notes or make a crib sheet while demonstrating the process.

Student activities: Have students
- Practice the process with other staff members, and then get feedback.
- Flow chart the process.
- Point out the critical differences involved in checking out or in different types of materials.

Follow-up: Merge library etiquette with circulation procedures, and discuss how to deal with difficult people or sensitive issues.

Evaluation: Does the student correctly and efficiently circulate library materials?
Does the student maintain a courteous relationship with the public?

Sample Magazine Check-out Procedure

In an effort to improve the magazine check-out procedure, follow the steps below:

1. Large envelopes with barcodes are located below the drawers at the circulation desk. Take an envelope.
2. Ask patron to complete the magazine check-out form as below:

Name	*Homeroom Teacher*		
Magazine Title	*month*	*day*	*year*
Magazine Title	*month*	*day*	*year*

3. Pull up patron record on computer.
4. Scan the barcode on the large envelope (see step 1) so that it records "periodicals" on the patron's record. Hit "Check Out."
5. Write the last three digits of the barcode on the upper right-hand corner of the magazine form, and on the upper right-hand corner of the inside first page of each magazine.
6. Place the magazines inside the envelope.
7. Stamp the envelope and the magazine form with the three day stamp.
8. Ask patron to please return all magazines at the same time in the same envelope.
9. File the magazine form below in its check-box, located to the right of the computer tower.

Sample Magazine Check-in Procedure

1. Find the magazine form that matches the last three digits of the barcode on the envelope.
2. Verify that all magazines have been returned.
   a. If some magazines are missing, cross off the returned magazines. Refile the magazine form.
      Place envelope in "Unreturned magazines" Princeton file until the remaining magazines are returned.
   b. If all magazines have been returned, throw away the form.
      Scan the barcode and hit "Check in."
      Place envelope in the pile of envelopes ready to check out.
4. If magazines are returned without the envelope, then check the magazine form. Follow step 2.
   [Note that you will need to manually type in the barcode number.
   All barcodes for periodicals begin with "3003," followed by the three digits on the form or magazine.]

Miscellaneous desk routines

Objectives:	The student will efficiently perform miscellaneous functions at the main desk.
Process:	The trainer describes different situations that occur at the desk, and models how to deal with them. The student practices the procedures, and asks clarifying questions as needed.
Demonstration ideas:	• Follow the steps enumerated in the circulation process above. • Have the student shadow an expert desk monitor, who talks through the process either during the transaction or immediately after. • Brainstorm with the student a list of miscellaneous routines, and together create a decision flow chart for each task. Here are some sample ones: reserves, change, IOUs, fines, lending supplies, getting donations, phone calls, giving directions, passes and sign-ins, opening and closing.
Student activities:	Have students • Make crib notes for the various routines. • Make a flow chart for each task. • Role-play the various transactions with other staff as coaches.
Follow-up:	Explain how staff often deal with several different tasks, one right after the other, at the main desk. Discuss with the student how to prioritize the transactions.
Evaluation:	Does the student • Handle the various main desk routines efficiently? • Maintain a calm and courteous demeanor while working at the desk? • Effectively prioritize sometimes competing tasks?

Priority Exercise for Main Desk Tasks

Six people come up to you at the main desk. Each has a different request.

1. Student A is in a rush, and wants change for the copier.

2. Teacher B hands you a dozen books she wants reserved for next period.

3. Student C wants to borrow a pair of scissors.

4. Teacher D wants to sign up to use the library next period.

5. Student E needs a hall pass to go to the bathroom.

6. John Q. Public comes in with two bags of books to donate.

Prioritize them.

Then Student A says the copier is jammed.

And YOU need to go to the bathroom.

And the phone rings.

[Each site may have different priorities so the library staff must determine the appropriate actions.]

Dewey Decimal Classification

Objective:

The student will explain the rationale of book arrangement, and can predict the subject of a book based on its DDC number.

Process:

The trainer explains the underlying principles of the DDC system and gives concrete examples of typical call numbers. Note that in-depth knowledge of the DDC system is not needed in order to perform most student-level library tasks. The best way to learn the DDC system is to come into contact with it during different functions shelving, processing, discarding, research).

Demonstration ideas:

- Develop a self-paced guide sheet that explains the DDC system.
- Develop or use an existing HyperCard card (available from the author) about the DDC system. Have the student complete the tutorial.
- Develop or use commercial diagrams about the DDC system.
- Classify books, and discuss with the student how the DDC number was assigned.
- Share DDC reference books, and show how the system was developed and how it works.

Student actvities:

Have the student
- Given a list of titles, assign the appropriate DDC number.
- Given uncatalogued books, assign the appropriate DDC number.
- Given a DDC number, predict the subject matter.

Follow-up:

Connect the DDC system with shelving and book processing. Show how the student can use knowledge of the DDC system can to help other students research a topic.

Evaluation:

Can the student explain the relationship between the DDC number and the material at hand?

Dewey Decimal Classification System

DEWEY DECIMAL CLASSIFICATION SYSTEM

A classification system is used to arrange materials in the library for easy access.

The **Dewey Decimal Classification System** is one of the oldest and most widely used systems.

◁ Go Back | Help! | Map | Main Menu | QUIT | Continue ▷

Dewey Decimal Classification System

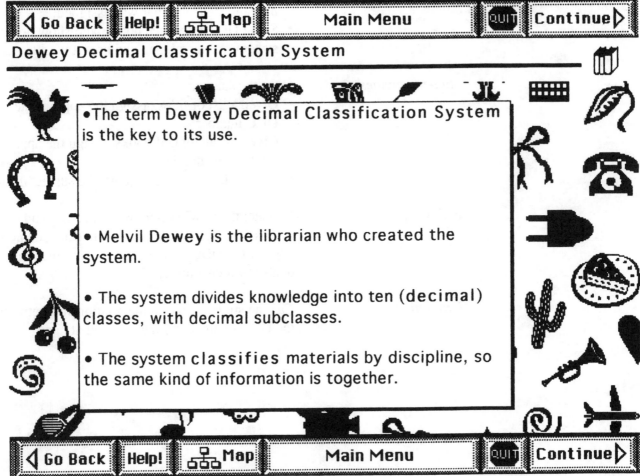

•The term **Dewey Decimal Classification System** is the key to its use.

• Melvil **Dewey** is the librarian who created the system.

• The system divides knowledge into ten (decimal) classes, with decimal subclasses.

• The system classifies materials by discipline, so the same kind of information is together.

◁ Go Back | Help! | Map | Main Menu | QUIT | Continue ▷

Dewey Decimal Classification System

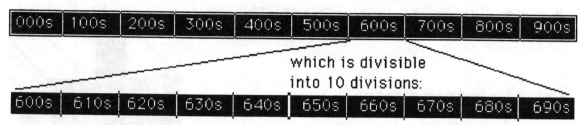

- Each discipline or subject is divided into 10 classes:

| 000s | 100s | 200s | 300s | 400s | 500s | 600s | 700s | 800s | 900s |

which is divisible
into 10 divisions:

| 600s | 610s | 620s | 630s | 640s | 650s | 660s | 670s | 680s | 690s |

which can be further subdivided into sections for very specific topics.

> For example,
>
> **click on each number**
>
> 600   is Technology (Applied sciences)
> 630   is Agriculture and related sciences
> 636   is Animal husbandry
> 636.1 is Horses

◁ Go Back | Help! | Map | Main Menu | QUIT | Continue ▷

Dewey Decimal Classification System

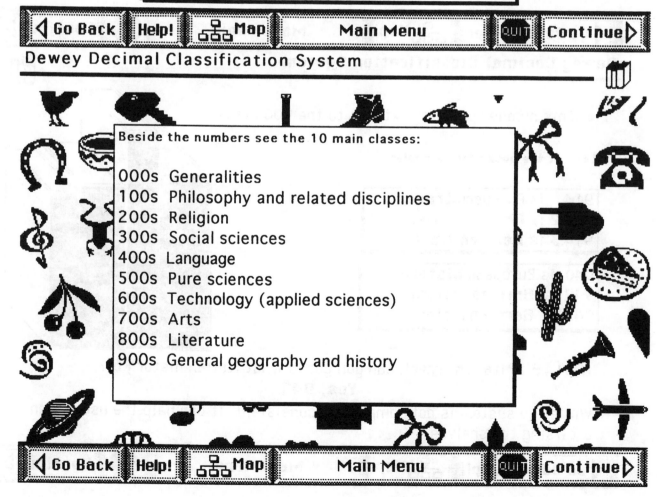

> **Beside the numbers see the 10 main classes:**
>
> 000s Generalities
> 100s Philosophy and related disciplines
> 200s Religion
> 300s Social sciences
> 400s Language
> 500s Pure sciences
> 600s Technology (applied sciences)
> 700s Arts
> 800s Literature
> 900s General geography and history

◁ Go Back | Help! | Map | Main Menu | QUIT | Continue ▷

Dewey Decimal Classification System (DDC)

Dewey Decimal Classification System

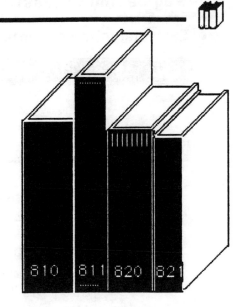

• Some classes have special characteristics which make it easier to locate an item.

Look at the books for examples

800 is literature
810 is **American** literature
820 is **British** literature

811 is American **poetry**
821 is British **poetry**

If 830 is German literature, can you guess what 831 stands for?
Yes, German poetry.

◁ Go Back ┃ Help! ┃ ⬚ Map ┃ **Main Menu** ┃ QUIT ┃ Continue ▷

Dewey Decimal Classification System

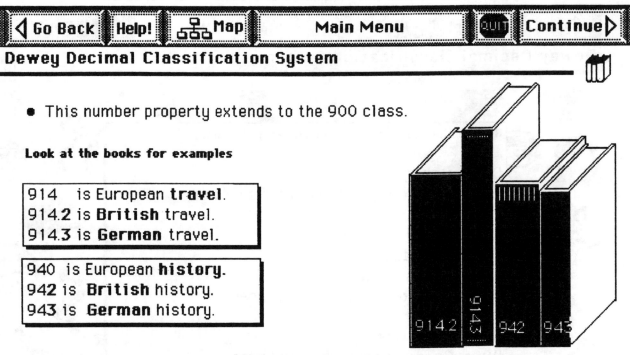

• This number property extends to the 900 class.

Look at the books for examples

914   is European **travel**.
914.2 is **British** travel.
914.3 is **German** travel.

940 is European **history**.
942 is **British** history.
943 is **German** history.

If 914.5 is Italian travel, can you guess what Italian history is?
Yes, 945.

While the system is not completely consistent, it can help the user when browsing the shelves.

◁ Go Back ┃ Help! ┃ ⬚ Map ┃ **Main Menu** ┃ QUIT ┃ Continue ▷

Dewey Decimal Classification System

- There may be more than one place to classify a book.

- For instance, "marriage" has ethical, religious, sociological, legal, and other aspects.

Look at the following classification numbers for possible books on marriage:

173	ethics of family relationships
241	moral theology
248.4	Christian marriage ceremony and practice
306.8	sociology of marriage
312	marriage statistics
346.01	laws related to marriage
362.8	marriage counseling
392	marriage customs

◁ Go Back | Help! | Map | Main Menu | QUIT | Continue ▷

Dewey Decimal Classification System Guide Sheets
U. S. Dept. of Education. College Library Technology and Cooperation, Computer-based Library Instruction Project, Washington, DC, 1994.

These and other HyperCard-produced guide sheets may be reproduced as is as transparencies to use as lecture notes when instructing students. DDC HyperCard stacks may be obtained from San Francisco State University's library c/o CLIP (Harriet Talan).

Dewey Decimal Classification Jeopardy

Directions: Give the DDC number for the following books:

Religions of Asia

Annotated Shakespeare

Space: the Last Frontier

New Encyclopedia

Psychology for the Millions

Inventions Today and Tomorrow

Our Indian Heritage

Techniques of Collage

Your Supreme Court at Work

Sign Language

Shelving principles and practices

Objectives:	The student will be able to shelve library materials accurately and efficiently.
Process:	The trainer explains the arrangement of books, then demonstrates each step in putting books in order and shelving them. Then the trainer models the shelving process for magazines and for other library materials. Exceptions to normal procedures (special collection, oversized books) should be highlighted during each step.
Demonstration ideas:	1. Walk through the first step of the process, verbally telling how to arrange books in order on a cart.
	2. Next, have students finish putting books in order on the cart, explaining how they decided the placement. Verbally coach the students as requested.
	3. With the book cart in order, start shelving the books into the main collection, verbally telling how to place them.
	4. Next, have students continue the process without comment. Give any suggestions afterwards.

5. Finally, have students independently put a cartload of books in correct shelf order. Check for accuracy. Have student shelve one range of books, tilting the books so the trainer can check them.
- Have students take notes or make a crib sheet while demonstrating the process.
- Instead of using real books in the steps above, use cardboard strips with various call numbers written on them.
- If the library has special spine labels or symbols, explain each one using the image and show on a map where each is shelved (mysteries, story collections, reference, foreign language, biographies, special series).

Student actvities:

Have the student
- Given a list of call numbers, put them in shelf order.
- Given a set of catalog cards, put them in shelf list order.
- Given overdue date-due cards, put them in shelf list order.

Follow-up:

Point out that shelving is connected to research strategies (browsing by call number). Discuss shelf lists and inventory procedures.

Evaluation:

Can the student shelve accurately and efficiently? Can the student accurately put catalog cards and datedue cards in shelf list order?

Shelving Rules

- Each book is labelled with a **call number**, which consists of the classification number and an author indicator.

- Call numbers may look like:

811 S	811 San	811 S23	811 Sa56	811 SAN

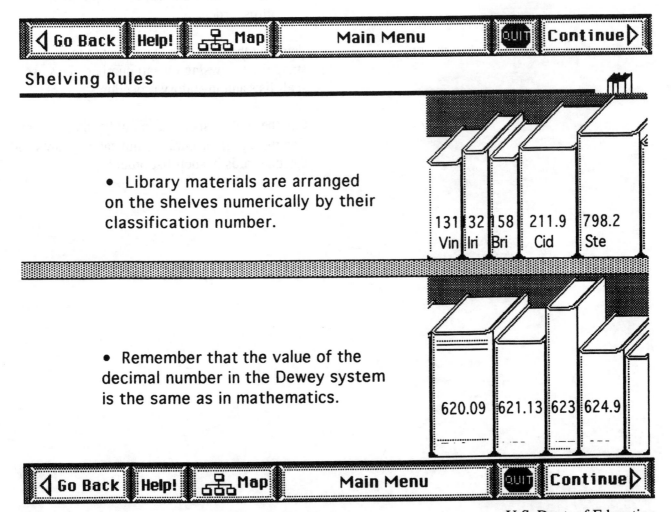

Harvest Poems by Carl Sand- burg

811 s23

Shelving Rules

- Library materials are arranged on the shelves numerically by their classification number.

131 Vin | 32 Iri | 158 Bri | 211.9 Cid | 798.2 Ste

- Remember that the value of the decimal number in the Dewey system is the same as in mathematics.

620.09 | 621.13 | 623 | 624.9

U.S. Dept. of Education

Filing principles

Objectives:	The student will file materials accurately.
Process:	Check the student's ability to alphabetize. Show filing rules.
Demonstration ideas:	• Model how to file catalog cards, and coach while the student files individual cards either with the real catalog or with a set of training cards.
	• Develop a sheet of filing rules, and have students refer to it while they file a set of training cards. Check the work.
	• Have students examine a book of subject headings, and have them generate a set of rules for filing.
	• Provide students with a self-paced guide on filing rules, and check results when they file a set of training cards. (See Diane Foxhill Carother's book *Self-instruction Manual for Filing Catalog Cards* by ALA, 1981.)
Student activities:	• Check student filing.
	• Have students compare word-by-word and letter-by-letter filing rules.
	• Have students correct misfiled drawers.
Follow-up:	Reinforce the fact that accurate filing is necessary for users to find the materials they need. Explain how computers file, and the differences between automated and human filing.
Evaluation:	Does the student file accurately and efficiently? Can the student explain the difference between word-by-word and letter-by-letter filing? Given a topic, can the student find a subject in the card catalog?

Library Catalogs

The library catalog's entries are filed <u>alphabetically</u>, by first line: either or .

Compare each method to see how they differ

Word by Word	Letter by Letter
San Antonio	San Antonio
San Diego	Sanctuary
San Pedro	Sandalwood
Sanctuary	Sand blasting
Sand blasting	Sand, George
Sand, George	San Diego
Sandalwood	San Pedro

◁ Go Back | Help! | 🖧 Map | **Main Menu** | QUIT | Continue ▷

Library Catalogs

The **card catalog** is the traditional catalog found in libraries. It is a group of cards filed alphabetically, and kept in drawers.

Card catalogs usually have one of two styles:
- **Dictionary:** all types of entries are filed together
- **Divided:** different types of entries are filed separately. The most common sections are: **author/title** and **subject**.

Inside tip:
A microform catalog (sometimes called COM) most closely resembles a card catalog.

◁ Go Back | Help! | 🖧 Map | **Main Menu** | QUIT | Continue ▷

Filing principles

Library Catalogs

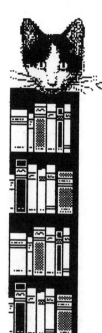

There are separate, specific filing rules for Author-Title entries filed word by word:
- Articles at the beginning of titles are ignored. (examples: a, an, the)
- Punctuation marks for corporate entries are ignored.
- Author names are inverted, and filed by last name.
- Sources by the same author are listed alphabetically by title.
- Acronyms are interfiled with initials.
- Abbreviations are filed as though spelled out. (example: Mr. is filed as Mister)
- Numbers are filed as though spelled out.

◁ Go Back | Help! | 🔲 Map | Main Menu | QUIT | Continue ▷

Library Catalogs

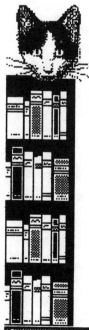

There are separate, specific filing rules for Subject entries filed word by word:
- Sources on the same subject are listed alphabetically by the main entry.
- Time and Period subdivisions are filed by date.

Complex subject headings may be filed in this order:
- One-word headings first
- Dash after one word next (example: China–Art)
- Period next (example: China. Army)
- Comma next (example: China, West)
- Phrases last (example: China Sea)

◁ Go Back | Help! | 🔲 Map | Main Menu | QUIT | Continue ▷

Procedures for making notices

Objectives: The student will generate accurate notices and distribute them efficiently.

Process: Provide students with a sample notice form, and give them the information needed to complete the form. Show them how to sort and distribute the notices.

Demonstration ideas:
- Guide the student through the steps of generating notices:
  Determine who needs the notice (e.g., overdues, reserve).
  Choose the proper form.
  Transfer the appropriate information onto the form.
  Sort the forms (usually by homeroom teacher or students' last name).
  Show how to distribute the forms (mailroom or other school delivery system).
- Have the student shadow an experienced notice maker.
- Have the student take notes or make a crib sheet for notice procedures.

Student activities:
- Have the student create a select group of notices, and check the results.
- Have teachers report whether they received the notices, and state how well they were done.

Follow-up: Explain how notices link with inventory and legal issues. Show how accurate shelving relates to accurate notice generation.

Evaluation: Does the student write clearly and accurately?
Does the student accurately transcribe the information from one form onto another?
Can the student accurately generate notices using a computerized circulation program?

Sample Notice Procedure Generated from a Circulation Program (Winnebago)

1. Enter the Reports menu.

2. Check that the printer is on.

3. Click on the Overdues option.

4. Select the following options:
   Send Report Data to: **Printer**
   Print: **Range**
   Report size: **3"x5"**
   Fields: **include user-defined, exclude address**
   Limit Report by number of days: **1 to 999**
   [Press F10]
   Remake Sort File: **Yes**
   Index Report by: **user field #3**
   Subsort by: **Patron's last name**
   [Press F10]

5. Print function is activated. WAIT!

6. When printout is finished, cut notices apart, and staple them together by homeroom teacher.

7. Place overdue notices in teachers' mailboxes.

Inventory procedures

Objectives:	The student will inventory the library's collection accurately and efficiently.
Process:	The trainer explains the rationale behind taking inventory. The trainer then shows how inventory is taken and coaches the student's efforts.
Demonstration ideas:	• Flow-chart the inventory process. • Have the student shadow experienced inventory takers. • Have the student simulate the inventory process.
Student activities:	Have the student • Inventory a limited part of the collection, and check results. • Buddy with an experienced inventory taker. • Develop a procedures guide for taking inventory.
Follow-up:	With the student, develop a flow chart that links inventory, notices, shelving, and ordering procedures.
Evaluation:	Do students inventory accurately and efficiently: are the items that they say are on the shelves really there; are items that they says are missing truly lost? Does the student know how to handle materials that are out of order but still in the library?

Sample Library Inventory Process

Legend: SL = Shelflist;   CF = Circulation file

1. Go to shelf with appropriate section of SL.

2. Read titles and author from SL card.

3. a. If book IS on shelf, compare information on SF to book.
   i. If all information matches, drop card into SL file.
   ii. Otherwise, write note describing discrepency and give book and SL to staff.
   b. If book is NOT on shelf, flip SL card up.

4. Repeat steps 1-3 until SL section is completed.

5. Take completed SL section to CF.

6. Compare flipped SF with book cards in CF.

7. a. If title IS in CF, drop card into SL file.
   b. If title is NOT in CF, compare flipped SF with reserved books.
   i. If book IS in reserve section, drop card into SL file.
   ii. If book is NOT in reserve section, clip remaining flipped SL with marker.

8. Proceed with next SF section, and repeat steps 1-7.

Processing

Getting library materials ready for use and keeping them in good shape are central functions within the library. These are tasks which students usually like to engage in because they see immediate results—and because they get the first chance to look at the new goodies! In a way, the processes associated with library resources manifest a kind of life cycle, from acquisition to discarding—with healthy use in between.

In considering processing, some underlying principles exist for acquiring, maintaining, and withdrawing library holdings. Each requires careful consideration and evaluation. Is a book worth mending? Does a particular magazine merit renewal? At what point should a filmstrip be tossed? The librarian usually makes these decisions, but the student can help in carrying out the decision's implications.

Books and magazines each require specialized ways of handling. Because library materials get heavy use (hopefully), a strong program of materials preparation can extend the life of these important resources.

Audiovisual materials usually get different treatment because they often require special equipment to use them. Additionally, these formats are sometimes more fragile than print items. Nor can one reinforce videotapes or slides to the same degree that books can be preserved.

Likewise, the ephemeral nature of vertical and pamphlet files raises the issue of preservation: When should clippings be tossed? When do "hot" topics become cold—and laid to rest? Student help can support the library's policies relative to vertical files, especially because students can provide a reality check as to the currency of a subject.

Computer programs also need processing, though in a unique way. Generally, programs aren't useful until they are copied or loaded onto a machine. Because software is routinely upgraded, or needs regular technical reference help, registration and documentation are crucial.

While preventive care is the best insurance for long-lasting library holdings, items do require repairs upon occasion. Student staff can do simple tasks that can prolong an important resource and get it into the hands of more users.

General acquisitions procedures

Objectives:	The student will explain the basis upon which the librarian selects materials to be added to the collection, and the process whereby they are acquired. The student will explain his/her role in this process.
Process:	The trainer, preferably the librarian, shows the student the selection policy and discusses how materials are selected. The trainer shares ways that materials are requested and reviewed. The trainer shows the ordering process, from budget to purchase orders. The trainer and student discuss how the student might get involved in the acquisitions process: by suggesting titles, by reviewing, or by typing up order forms.

Demonstration ideas:

- Develop a flow chart of decision points in acquisitions.
- Gather a set of policies and forms that relate to acquisitions, and explain how each is used.
- Trace a library item from request/review to shelf, and show the student the steps along the way.
- Have the student read reviews and write original ones.

Follow-up:	Encourage students to have a say in purchases. Have them suggest acquisition items, and discuss their viability.
Evaluation:	Can the student explain the underriding principles of acquisitions? Can the student identify criteria for material inclusion in the library?

Steps and Issues in Acquiring Materials

1. Check budget for adequate funding.
   - If one category of spending is over-budget, can you transfer funds?
   - If funds are inadequate, what other funding sources are available?

2. Prepare purchase order.
   - Include as much bibliographic information as possible (e.g., author, title, publisher, date, ISBN, local order number, quantity, cost).
   - Does order need to be prepaid?
   - Does the order need a purchase order number?
   - Does the order have a deadline, especially for sales?

3. Select supplier.
   - Comparison shop among jobbers, publishers, distributor (e.g., bookstore).
   - Take into consideration costs for: handling, shipping, taxes.
   - Consider options such as standing orders and book clubs.

4. Send order.
   - Is batch ordering more efficient or cost-effective?
   - What time deadlines exist? (e.g., does a teacher need a book tomorrow?)

5. Record expenses.
   - Expense is immediately embumbered.
   - Pay only upon receipt.
   - Note that some shipments may arrive in multiple packages and different times.

6. Receive materials.
   - Check packing slip to make sure it it accurate.
   - Check items for damages. (Return damaged materials, and record transaction.)
   - Send invoice for proper payment.
   - Process items.

General concepts of maintenance

Objectives:

The student will be able to care for library materials.

Process:

The trainer explains the principles of maintenance: to prolong the useful life of a library holding. The trainer introduces the student to basic procedures related to maintenance, such as careful handling of material and referral of damaged items to a repair center.

Demonstration ideas:

- Show a book or magazine in good condition and one in damaged condition, and explain how maintenance can affect their physical conditions.
- Show the cost of replacing books, and explain how preventive maintenance can make it possible to use money to purchase new titles rather than replace old ones.
- Have the student shadow a good repair person and learn the necessary skills.

Student activities:

Have the student
- Create a do's and don'ts list of maintenance practices.
- Diagnose at-risk library materials.

Follow-up:

- Link maintenance with acquisitions and withdrawals so students can see the interrelations of the tasks.

Evaluation:

Does the student handle library materials responsibly?
At the point that an item needs to be repaired, does the student signal the appropriate person or put the damaged item where it can be repaired?

Maintenance Tips:

Reinforce books:
1. Using one inch of fiber tape, place the tape alongside the top edge and alongside the bottom edge of the inside front page, and the inside back page, of the book with each piece centered on the crease.
2. Grasp all of the book pages, letting the hardback cover fall to the surface. Gently release and crease 20 pages, front and back, at a time until the center is reached.

Reinforce magazines:
1. Using one inch of fiber tape, place the tape alongside the top edge and alongside the bottom edge of the inside front page, and the inside back page, of the magazine with each piece centered on the crease
2. Using one inch of transparent book tape, place the tape along the spine of the magazine, centered on the edge.

Dry-mount articles and pictures:
1. Use acid-free stock paper, preferably letter size.
2. Apply rubber cement to the back of the item and to the corresponding front area of the stock paper.
3. Adhere the item to the stock paper. Allow to dry. If needed, put the dry mounted item under a heavy weight for a day.

Shelving practices:
1. Retrieve a book by gently pushing back on the two surrounding books, and pulling out the desired book by grasping the entire spine. Never pull by the top of the book spine.
2. Never jam a shelf. Instead, shift the shelf's books to make room for the volume you are trying to shelve.
3. Ideally, either space shelving to accommodate the biggest book, or shelve oversized books. A good method is to reserve a narrow shelf on top for oversized books, which can be shelved horizontally. If an oversized book has to be shelved in "tipped" fashion, lay it on its spine rather than on its far edges.

Storing nonprint items:
1. Aim for a low-humidity or air-conditioned environment.
2. Do not expose items to bright, prolonged light.
3. Containers should be acid-free.
4. Store posters and charts flat rather than rolled up. Use large, shallow drawers to prevent posters from being rifled through.
5. Place slides in plastic pocketed binders or in trays.

General principles and procedures for withdrawals

Objectives:
The student will follow withdrawal procedures accurately and efficiently.

Process:
The trainer explains each step in withdrawing a library item, particularly books: eliminating it from the circulation program, the card catalog, the shelf list, the accession book; and marking the item as discarded. At each step the trainer has the student perform the task, and coaches as needed.

Demonstration ideas:
1. Walk through the first specific step.
2. Next, have the student walk through the first step, explaining it. Coach as needed.
3. Next have the student do the process independently, and give any suggestions afterwards.
4. Repeat with each step.
- Have the student take notes or make a crib sheet while demonstrating the process.
- Show students the criteria for withdrawing an item. Then give them some potential titles to withdraw and have them decide how to deal with the item, justifying their decisions.

Student activities:
- Have the student flow chart the withdrawal process.
- Given a set of books and other materials, and have them decide whether to keep, repair, or discard them and justify their decision.
- Withdraw a select group of items. Ask the trainer or librarian to check how well it was done.

Follow-up:
Link withdrawals to acquisitions.

Evaluation:
Can the student withdraw an item accurately and completely?
Can the student identify items that should be withdrawn?

Sample Checklist for Withdrawing an Item from the Library

☐ Mark item as withdrawn. Cross out or erase all library markings.
☐ Remove copy from shelflist. If item is the last one, then remove card set from card catalog.
☐ Remove copy from accession record.
☐ Remove copy from circulation program. Recycle barcode, if possible.
☐ Replace item if needed.

Book processing procedures

Objectives: The student will process books accurately and efficiently.

Process: The trainer explains the rationale for book processing: to get materials ready for active use. The trainer then demonstrates and explains each step in processing a book, taking time to have the student practice at each step. The trainer explains process variations for different types of books. The librarian may decide to have student staff specialize in a few steps of the entire process (for example, just covering paperbacks). Note that students can perform most book processing steps. The keys are student capability and interest, thorough training, and librarian trust and ability to delegate and supervise.

Demonstration ideas: 1. Walk through the entire process once, verbally explaining each specific step.
2. Have students try doing the first step in the process, verbally coaching them along the way.
3. Have students do the process as they explain how to do it. Coach as needed.
4. Have the student practice the process. Assess process and products afterwards.
• Make a video of the book processing "cycle."
• Create a set of process cards (4"x6" or 5"x7"). Number each card. Laminate the set, double hole-punch them on the top, and put them on metal rings. The set may be taken apart to guide each step. The set can also be used during demonstrations as a visual aid to flow-charting the process.

Nonprint processing, storage, and maintenance procedures

Objectives: The student will process nonprint resources effectively.

Process: The trainer demonstrates each step in processing nonprint material, storing it, and maintaining it.

Demonstration ideas:

1. Walk through the check-in process, describing each step.
2. Next, have the student walk through the process, saying aloud each step. Verbally coach the student as requested.
3. Next, have the student walk through the process without comment. Give any suggestions afterwards.

• Demonstrate the full cycle of nonprint item: from ordering to processing to maintenance to withdrawal.

• Show how the maintenance of nonprint affects its accompanying equipment and vice versa.

Student activities:

Have the student

• Draw a map tracing nonprint material from acquisition to shelving.

• Match the nonprint material with its associated piece of equipment and explain how the maintenance of each is essential to the overall condition of both.

• Compare nonprint processing with the processing of other formats.

Follow-up: Link nonprint processing with processing in other formats; link nonprint processing with equipment usage and maintenance.

Evaluation: Does the student process nonprint items accuragely?
Can the student compare nonprint processing with processing of other media?
Can the student explain the relationship of equipment maintenance and nonprint maintenance?

Sample Guide Sheet for Processing Computer Software

1. Check packing slip.

2. Check container (box, envelope) to make sure no disks or documentation are missing.

3. Mark all documentation on the front cover with the library stamp.

4. Place a library sticker on all disks.

5. Copy all disks and label them as archive copies.

6. Copy the registration number of all disks onto the main documentation.

7. Register the software and photocopy the completed registration (including the registration number).

8. Place all pieces of the package in their correct place:
    - Container into office container shelves alphabetically,
    - Registration/warranty original into "to mail" box,
    - Registration/warranty photocopy into office file under "Computer software warranty,"
    - Packing slip into office file under "Finance—packing slips," and
    - Original disks into library technician's box,
    - Archive disks into office software drawer alphabetically.

9. Classify and catalog software.

Vertical file processing, classification, storage, and maintenance

Objectives:
- The student will identify possible vertical file resources.
- The student will select relevant articles and classify them appropriately. The student will clip, label, and mount articles and pictures accurately and efficiently.
- The student will correctly classify and accurately label pamphlets and other vertical file materials.
- The student will store vertical file materials accurately, carefully, and efficiently.
- The student will discard vertical file items appropriately and efficiently.

Process:

The trainer explains the rationale for vertical files, the variety of resource formats, and the basis for their processing and maintenance. Each step is demonstrated, and the student practices it.

Demonstration ideas:
- Walk through the entire process once, explaining each step.
- Have the students try doing the first step in the process, verbally coaching them along the way.
- Have students do the process as they explain how to do it. Coach as needed.
- Have the student practice the process. Assess process and products afterwards.
- Pull out several vertical file folders and discuss why the sources were chosen and how they were processed.
- Using an authority file (i.e., vertical file subject list), discuss with the student how topics are chosen and materials classified under the headings.
- Make a video of the vertical file processing "cycle."

Student activities:

Have the student
- Classify a set of pre-clipped articles.
- Discard outdated or worn vertical file items.
- Examine a copy of *PAIS* or government consumer catalog and choose potential vertical file items.

Follow-up: Link vertical file selection with general collection development policies. Link vertical file classification with book classification and magazine indexing. Link vertical file discarding with withdrawal procedures for other types of library resources.

Evaluation: Can the student
- List different types of vertical file items?
- Correctly classify vertical file items?
- Carefully and accurately prepare vertical file items for storage?
- Purge a vertical file folder effectively?

Sample Flow Chart for Vertical File (VF) Processing

VF = Vertical File

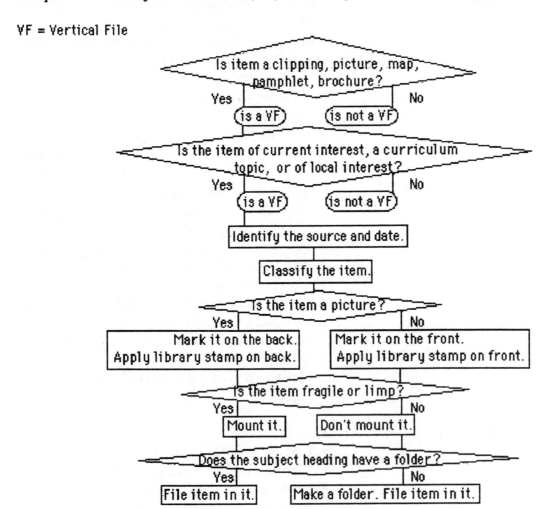

Repairs

Objectives:

The student will be able to perform simple repairs accurately and efficiently.

Process:

The trainer explains the rationale behind repairing. The trainer demonstrates various repair procedures, giving students the opportunity to practice skills in repairing.

Demonstration ideas:

1. Walk through the entire process once, explaining each step.
2. Have students try doing the first step in the process, coaching them along the way.
3. Have students do the process and explain it as they do it. Coach as needed.
4. Have students practice the process. Assess process and products afterwards.
- Videotape repair procedures.
- Have the student shadow a repair expert in another library.
- Produce repair guidesheets for each kind of repair.

Student activities:

- As students shelve materials, have them identify items for repair, determining which materials merit repair and which should be discarded.
- Have them produce a decision chart for repairs.

Follow-up:

Discuss levels of repairing: simple vs professional, and when to rebind or discard materials. Discuss preventive maintanence.

Evaluation:

Can the student
- Correctly determine when a library item needs repair?
- Perform simple repairs accurately and efficiently?
- Determine when an item needs professional repairing or discarding?

Sample Book Repair Checklist

☐ Spot potential repairs early, such as
    ☐ pages (torn, soiled, detached, missing)
    ☐ cover (warped, soiled, torn spine, bent corners)
    ☐ cover-page connection (detached, loose)

☐ Determine repair option:
    ☐ simple repair
    ☐ expert repair
    ☐ rebind
    ☐ discard
    ☐ conserve (for archival, historic reasons, for instance)

☐ Gather repair materials.

☐ Follow repair guidelines.

☐ Work carefully, accurately, neatly, thoroughly.

☐ Apply preventive measures to forestall further repairs. (Gale 3-7)

Use of Equipment and Technology

Equipment has always played a part in the school library: from the stamper to the barcode scanner, from the pencil sharpener to the photocopier, from the slide projector to the multimedia computer station. Today, library equipment continues to augument librarian productivity and student learning. But the variety of equipment and the knowledge base needed in order to operate and maintain all of it has grown tremendously over the last few years.

Library student staff have, by and large, lived with equipment from infancy. Most of them are not intimidated by technology; they are more likely to explore and take risks with machines than many librarians may be comfortable with. As librarians channel these natural tendencies and train students to improve library service through technology, they facilitate student growth as well as get needed help in delivering resources to library users.

As with the other library tasks, training students in equipment use and operation should underscore the library's mission. Equipment is a means to information and ideas, not an end in itself (compelling as that concept can be to some youth). The librarian must insist on careful handling, documentation of all system modification and repairs, and constructive use of equipment. Student staff should also be expected to help other people learn how to operate equipment properly so they too can access and process the information they need.

Because equipment operation, maintenance and trouble-shooting demand technical competence and responsibility, librarians often assign an elite crew to act as equipment specialists. Moreover, because classroom teachers occasionally need immediate technical help, the librarian can give these crew members special Tech Crew cards to give them access where teachers need instant assistance. Especially for middle schoolers, earning such a card is a high honor. The card can be a recruitment tool to broaden the base of technical helpers.

General strategies for using computer hardware

Objectives:

The student will
- Identify parts of the computer and associated devices (e.g., input, output, other peripherals).
- Operate the system and its devices (start, use, and shut down).
- Connect and disconnect computer system devices
- Perform basic functions using the computer's operating system: open, close and save files; use the desktop; print.
- Take care of hardware properly.

Process:

- The trainer explains the basic features of computer hardware, both the main system and associated devices, and how they relate.
- The trainer demonstrates how to operate each piece of equipment and has the student practice those operations.
- The trainer connects and disconnects system components and lets the student practice those skills.
- The trainer demonstrates how to care for computer hardware and has the student practice safe and careful procedures.

Demonstration ideas:

- Trace a computer function, such as word processing, in terms of all the devices involved. Start with the first electrical impulse and follow it throughout all of the connections.
- Open up a system to show the actual components: hard drive, CPU, RAM, video card, power supply. Walk through a computer process.
- Produce or use an existing videotape on computer systems and devices.
- Create FAQ sheets or guide cards about hardware operations and use.
- Have the student use a computer- or text-based tutorial.

Student activities:	Have the student • Diagram a computer system and its associated devices. • Act out the different parts of a computer or operating system, including peripherals. • Flow chart a computer process, noting all the operations and devices involved. • Create a chart that compares two computer systems (e.g., IBM vs Macintosh) in terms of hardware and operating systems. • Physically dissect a "dead" system and label each piece, then put it back together. • Diagram safe and unsafe practices. • Develop safety lab rules.
Follow-up:	Compare computer systems, discuss trouble-shooting strategies, link hardware to software issues, compare operating systems and utility programs.
Evaluation:	Can the student • Identify computer features and components? • Perform basic computer hardware functions? • Perform basic operating system tasks? • Accurately diagnose typical system problems? • Accurately and safety connect and disconnect devices? • Show safe and unsafe practices relative to hardware use?

Care and Maintenance of Hardware

Follow Instructions that come with any hardware or equipment.

Safe Practices:
- Handle all equipment carefully. Avoid sudden movements, such as jostling. Do not pull on cables or any other cords.
- Turn off all equipment before connecting or disconnecting parts.
- Keep sharp instruments away from equipment.
- Don't force anything into a port or other opening.
- Do not open equipment.
- Keep equipment away from wet, hot, cold, and dusty areas.
- Do not eat or drink near equipment.
- Clean outside cases with a damp cloth.
- Clean screens with a lint-free towel sprayed with glass cleaner.
- Cover equipment overnight.

Sample Computer Maintenance Kit

In a lunch box or carrying caddy, place the following items:
- Soft, lint-free cloth
- Q-tips
- Lint brush (to clean mousepad)
- Used fabric softener sheets to reduce static electricity on screens
- Denatured alcohol
- Spray bottle of glass cleaner
- Small clear plastic bags for storage
- Small flathead screwdriver
- Small Phillips screwdriver (Onishi)

General strategies for operating software

Objectives: The student will use a set of generic protocols to approach learning or operating an electronic resource.

Process: The trainer demonstrates how to use several pieces of software, explaining general functions common to most electronic software. The trainer then points out generic protocols or strategies used in learning how to use an electronic resource. The trainer compares protocols across computer system platforms and other equipment types.

Demonstration ideas:
- Demonstrate the use of a specific electronic resource in terms of its functions (e.g., search, print, save).
- Have the student try using a similar type of resource, explaining how to figure out main functions; coach as needed.
- Have student try using another type of electronic resource, and check how well protocols transfer.
- Produce a "walk-through" sheet that enables the student to discover basic program protocols.

Student activities: Have the student
- Compare several guide sheets or "how to" references in terms of generic computer protocols.
- Make a chart comparing general protocols (e.g., open, close, print, save) across computer platforms (PC vs Mac) or resource format (e.g., CD-ROM vs laser disc).
- Write computer "tips" for general machine use.
- Using screen "dumps" and word processing, make guide sheets for use with different electronic resources.

Follow-up: Link electronic resource use to more technical functions such as installing programs. Link use to peer teaching opportunities and general research strategies. Link concept of protocols to other media.

Evaluation: Given an electronic resource, can the student use it effectively?
Can the student explain basic features and functions of various electronic resources?
Can the student compare protocols across system platforms?

Generic Protocols for Electronic Resources

Menus

Menus act as tables of contents.

They are located on the opening screen or along one edge of screen.

Main menus often divide into more specific sub-menus.

Menus can refer to different topics, approaches, or computer functions.

A menu bar at top of screen is often called a *navigation* or *pull-down* bar.

To use, click on the term and drag the mouse down to the desired highlighted option.

Sometimes, the option can be activated by pressing a function key and letter simultaneously (e.g., ctrl-C).

Function Keys

Function keys are non-alphanumeric keys that allow the user to perform certain tasks.

Sample keys: enter, control, delete, tab, alternate, page up, page down, arrows, option, command, print screen, caps lock, number lock, escape.

Some keyboards include "F" keys, usually F1 to F10 or F12. These are located at the left or top of the keyboard. They are often program-specific, and enable to user to perform tasks such as print or save.

Sometimes the user has to press two keys simultaneously to activate the action, such as "ctrl-alt-del" to reboot a DOS computer system.

HELP is a special function. It might be activated by F1 or "command-H." Help can range from tips for a specific screen to an electronic tutor tour of an entire program. Sometimes Help is available at the specific point of need; sometimes it is one general screen of hints.

Printing

Most electronic resources let the user print the information.

The printer command is located in menu bar, usually under "File" or at the bottom of the screen as a function key (e.g., F6)

Usually, a portion of an entry can be printed by highlighting it and using either a "Print selection" option or going to the print dialog box where a "Print selection" option may be chosen.

If an option is greyed (e.g., not in black type and not possible to highlight), then it can't be done. This happens sometimes when the user wants to print a picture.

If something doesn't print, look for these common situations:
- The printer is off.
- The printer is not connected to the computer.
- The printer is out of paper.
- The wrong printer has been chosen.
- If several computers are linked to one printer, it make take a while for the printer to get to the job at hand.
- The printer driver has not been installed (least likely and most technical reason).

Searching

Browse searches alphabetically like an index. This approach works when the user doesn't know the exact wording or spelling (e.g., "Michelangelo").

Basic Search allows the user to type in a word for the computer to match with words in the program and retrieve the searched-for information. This approach works when the user has a simple topic to search or wants to see how a topic is related to other similar ones (e.g., "television").

Boolean Search allows the user to type several words or phrases together, linking them with *AND,OR*, or *NOT*. This approach works when the user wants to narrow or broaden a topic—or to find a specific relationship between two concepts (e.g., "tigers" and "Siberia"). (Pappas 3,4)

General Installation Procedures

Macintosh
1. Insert first floppy disk or CD-ROM.
2. Double-click on disk/CD-ROM icon.
3. Double-click on *INSTALL* icon.
4. If disk-detection dialog box appears, click *YES* button to disengage check feature.
5. Click *INSTALL or EASY INSTALL* button unless directed to customize the installation.
6. Follow installation directions. Insert designated disks as directed.
7. *RESTART* system when installation is successfully completed.
8. Create back-up disks if so instructed by staff.
8. Store disks (or CD-ROM) in order.

Windows:
1. Insert first floppy disk or CD-ROM.
2. Start Windows.
3. Open Program Manager.
4. Open File Manager.
5. Choose *RUN* under the FILE menu.
6. Type *diskdrive letter*:\setup. Usually, the floppy drive letter is A. Usually, the CD-ROM drive is D. Then click *OK* button.
7. Follow installation instructions. Insert designated disks as directed.
7. *RESTART* system when installation is successfully completed.
8. Create back-up disks if so instructed by staff.
8. Store disks (or CD-ROM) in order.

Sample Guide Sheet: Operating Scanner
1. Turn scanner on first.
2. Turn computer on second.
3. Double-click on Hard drive icon.
4. Double-click on Scanner folder.
5. Double-click on Ofoto.
6. Click OK button.
7. Place document face down on scanner glass surface with the right-hand upper corner of the document lined up with the right-hand upper corner of the glass surface.
8. Make sure scan controls match example.
9. Click Prescan button.
10. Use the selection rectangle to select the area you wish to scan.
11. After selection is made, click Scan button.
12. Under File (top menu bar), choose Save As.
13. Type in the name of your file in the shaded area, and click Save button.
14. Under Image (top menu bar), choose Sharpen.
15. Under Image (top menu bar), choosen Focus to get a clear picture.
16. When finished, Save your file again.

General operational procedures for audiovisual equipment

Objectives:

The student will explain the generic operations for audiovisual equipment. The student will operate a selection of audio-visual equipment safely and efficiently.

Process:

The trainer explains basic operating principles of audiovisual machines. The trainer demonstrates how to run specific kinds and brands of equipment. Students practice skills. The librarian may assign aides to particular types of equipment as specialties.

Demonstration ideas:

• Produce videotapes on equipment operation.
• Create guide sheets or cards (with diagrams) on equipment operation.
• Develop learning stations so students can proceed round-robin to different areas and learn how to operate equipment.
• Give a pre-test to see if students can already operate equipment satisfactorily. Experts can coach peers.
• Label parts of the machine so the student can follow sequentially what needs to be done.

Student activities:

Have the student
• Create a flow chart for equipment use.
• Compare equipment use for different brands of the same type of equipment (e.g., 16 mm film projector).
• Do a skit on proper and improper equipment use.

Follow-up:

Link equipment use to trouble-shooting. Underscore the need for preventive maintenance (e.g., careful transport).

Evaluation:

Can the student
• Explain generic equipment operation and handling?
• Operate equipment efficiently and safely?
• Explain to a peer or teacher how to operate a piece of equipment?

Sample Equipment Circulation Guidelines

Check-out Procedures

Check out equipment only to teachers. Students may check out a piece of equipment for a teacher upon written permission. However, library student staff must transport the equipment.

Follow check-out procedures as with a book, scanning the equipment's barcode. If a piece of equipment is stored on a cart, the cart accompanies the equipment.

Transporting Equipment

Stay with the equipment at all times.

Hold onto the equipment securely.

If the piece of equipment is on a cart, have another person help you gently lift or guide the cart over any bumpy spots (such as a door "lip").

Deliver the equipment to a teacher, and set it where the teacher designates.

When transporting equipment back to the library, place it in its permanent storage space.

Considerations in Using Sound Equipment

For tape recorders, CD and record players, and sound projectors, sound quality is controlled by the following equipment features:
- Amplifier
- Volume control (including stereo balance)
- Tone control (including balance between treble and base)
- Speed.

Speaker placement can also affect the sound. Some general tips are:
- Place the speaker at ear level.
- Place the speaker in the corner of the room.
- If two speakers are used, spread them wide apart and have each face the listener. Balance the sound between the two speakers.

Quality of sound reproduction is affected by
- Quality of the original sound
- Conditions under which the sound is recorded and played back
- Quality of the recording device (e.g., ability to capture range and tone)
- Quality of the playback equipment (e.g., balance, speakers)
- Ability of the person operating the equipment.

Microphones, particular affect the quality of sound reproduction. Here are some tips:
- Use a unidirectional microphone when only one person is speaking.
- Use a lavalier or lapel microphone for one speaker who needs to move a lot.
- Use an omnidirectional microphone when taping a panel or group. Most built-in microphones are omnidirectional. Generally, the closer the speaker and the more the person faces the mike, the more likely the sound will be picked up.
- Test any microphone with the people who will be using it so sound adjustments can be made ahead of time.

General Principles in Using Overhead Projectors

Set-Up

- Set the projector on a flat surface at a comfortable height for the user.
- Loop the power cord once around a leg of the projector table, cart or stand before plugging it into the outlet. (This prevents the cord from being yanked out accidentally.)
- Set the projector at the desired distance from the screen or projecting surface. (The greater the distance, the larger the projection.)
- Focus the projector to get a clear image.
- Adjust the projector mirror to get the best placement. The image should be above most viewers' heads, yet not be so high that it becomes distorted (keystoned).
- Check the lighting level so the image does not look washed out.
- Turn off the machine when not using it. Some machines have an option that allows the light to turn off but the power to remain, thus saving bulb life.

Maintenance

- Cover the projector when not in use.
- Never leave any object on the transparency glass table.
- Clean the glass surfaces with a clean dry cloth. Window cleaner may be used if sprayed onto the cloth first.
- Hold the projector securely when transporting it on a cart. Do not let it bounce.

General Principles in Using Slide Projectors

Set-up

- Set the projector on a stable surface.
- Loop the power cord once around a leg of the projector table or cart, or stand before plugging it into the outlet. (This prevents the cord from being yanked out accidentally.)
- Attach the remote control device.
- If the projection lens is stored separately, carefully insert it into the projector.
- Place the slide tray in the correct starting position on the projector. For carousel projectors, the tray slot on the bottom should be aligned with the selection slot on the machine. Check the placement by testing a slide or two.
- Set the projector at the desired distance from the screen or projecting surface. (The greater the distance, the larger the projection.)
- Turn the projector focus knob the to get a clear image.
- Adjust the elevation knob to get the best placement. The image should be above most viewers' heads, yet not be so high that the image becomes distorted (keystoned).
- Check the lighting level so the image does not look washed out.
- Turn the lamp switch to the fan level when not projecting slides. Some machines have an low light option that can prolong bulb life.

Shut-down and Maintenance:

- Turn the lamp switch off but keep the fan going a little while after finishing the slide show. This allows the bulb to cool down.
- Remove the slide tray before turning off all the power unless you are certain that the tray and machine slots are aligned perfectly.
- Screw the elevation knob all the way back flush with the machine.
- Screw the lens all the way back flush with the machine, or remove it carefully if it is to be stored separately.
- Disconnect and wrap all cords carefully, and store them properly. Some projectors have a built-in storage space.
- Store the projector in a case, and transport it carefully.

General Principles in Using Videotape Players and Recorders

Set-up
- Set the videotape machine on a flat, stable surface.
- Attach the machine to the monitor before turning any equipment on.
- Loop the power cord once around a leg of the machine table, cart or stand before plugging it into the outlet. (This prevents the cord from being yanked out accidentally.)
- Adjust the monitor to make sure it is in the right mode and on the right channel.
- Be sure that the power is on before loading or unloading the video-cassette; never force the cassette into the opening.
- Load the cassette slowly, with the label side facing you and the window side facing up.
- If the tape loads from the top, gently press down on the eject mechanism to close it.

Maintenance
- Cover the machine when not in use.
- Keep the machine away from water or heat sources.
- Use a damp cloth to clean the VCR case, but do not use liquid or aerosal cleaners.
- Clean the recorder heads monthly using a videotape cleaner tape. Mark the tape each time you use it and note the number of uses it can safely perform.
- If a videocassette gets jammed in the machine, do not insert metal or other hard material into the equipment.
- A videocassette that becomes tangled or loose from its housing can often be retracted and corrected by pushing in the side tab near the tape's "door" and carefully tilting back that door. Then the tape can be rewound manually. This procedure is best done by a team of two aides.

General Principles in using Camcorders

Set-up

- Set up the tripod for stablest recording. Be sure that the leg extensions are in the locked position to prevent the tripod from collapsing. Tighten any handles or locks to allow for controllable movement but no sudden shifts.
- Set up the power adapter to conserve battery life. Attach the cable to the camcorder first, loop the cable once around the tripod leg to prevent its being yanked out. If an extension cord is used, attach the plug to one end at this point. Only then should an electrical plug be placed in the outlet.
- Check to make sure the power adapter is in the right mode; *on camera* if the image is being recorded directly "live," *on line* if the image is being recorded by jacks from another source (typically, a television). (The adapter is placed in *on line* mode also when the battery is being recharged.
- Secure the camcorder onto the tripod. Be sure to hold the equipment solidly while you attach it.
- Check to make sure the battery is correctly placed inside the camcorder.
- Match the lighting option button to the recording conditions: i.e., inside or outside lighting.
- Remove the lens cap. Make sure not to lose it.
- Insert the recording tape into the machine. Place it label up and out, and close the camcorder "door" gently.
- Check for white balance and focus just before recording.
- Do not speak, or even whisper, near the camcorder unless you want the sound to be recorded.
- If the camera is not being used, keep the lens cap on.

Maintenance

- Handle the camcorder carefully and gently.
- Always hold the camcorder securely.
- Store the camcorder in a sturdy, durable case between shoots.
- Never point the camera lens into the sun. It is wise to avoid pointing it at a television as well.
- Do not put fingers, jewelry, or other objects into the camcorder.
- Keep the camcorder away from water or heat sources.
- If you sense something wrong with the camera (smells, strange noises, smoke), turn it off immediately and report the problem to the staff.
- Recharge the battery as soon as it is "drained." Keep a charged battery handy.

General trouble-shooting procedures

Objectives: The student will identify equipment problems. The student will solve simple equipment problems and will refer more difficult problems to the proper person.

Process: The trainer explains general approaches to trouble-shooting equipment problems. The trainer discusses how to diagnose a problem and either solve it or refer it to someone who can. The trainer demonstrates and explains simple equipment repairs.

Demonstration ideas:
- Describe case studies about equipment problems and discuss how to solve them.
- Share an equipment problem and demonstrate step-by-step how to solve it.
- Create guide sheets or cards for simple equipment repairs.
- Produce a videotape on simple troubleshooting techniques.
- Have the student shadow a technician to learn how to troubleshoot equipment.

Student activities: Have the student
- Videotape sample training sessions.
- Create a trouble-shooting decision flow chart.
- Compare repair techniques for different kinds of equipment and identify common trouble-shooting techniques.
- Diagnose equipment problems, and explain what action to take.

Evaluation: Can the student
- Correctly diagnose an equipment problem?
- Decide on appropriate actions to take relative to equipment problems?
- Do simple equipment repairs that enable the machine to operate well afterwards?

Sample Equipment Program Report Form

Name: Room: Date:
Station number (if applicable):

Did you check:
Is the electricity working (outlet, switch, power strip)?
Is it plugged in?
Are all the connections OK and secure?
Is it turned on?

For printers:
Is there paper?
Is there enough ink (toner, cartridge, ribbon)?
Is the right printer chosen on the computer system?

System questions:
Is the problem local to one machine?
Is the problem consistent or is it intermittent?
Does the problem exist for all software resources or just one?

Equipment:
Type of machine: Brand: Model:
Part of machine having trouble:

Description of problem:
When did it happen?
What happened at the time that the problem occurred?
What does the problem look like?
What did you do to correct the problem? What happened?
How urgent is the problem?

Action:
Date/time form received:
Who fixed problem: Date/time fixed:
Solution:

Reference Skills

All too often librarians limit library student staff to clerical chores. As a result, students don't learn the core skills that enable a library to use its resources effectively. Particularly since student staff represent the library, and their peers intuitively consult them for library help, it behooves the librarian to reinforce basic reference skills routinely given to all students as well as to teach student staff some advanced tools and strategies.

Probably the easiest and most natural way to begin this task is to guide student staff in their own research work. The critical difference is that the training is double-edged: The student learns both the reference skill *and* the reference process and instructional method used to teach it. That is, students learn how to teach the skill they are learning a sure-fire way for students to get a concept under their belts. Additionally, each training session should end with processing: How did the student feel about the training? What skills were easy to learn? What were the stumbling blocks? How would the student teach peers differently?

Another simple way to train student staff reference skills is to have them shadow the librarian. Whether the period includes class instruction or individual help, if the student staff listen attentively and take notes about the content and the strategy, they can discuss the process with the librarian sometime during that session. The essential questions are "What did you learn about reference skills?" "What techniques can you apply when helping others?"

If student staff finish their assigned work, and there's actually a "free" moment for them, the librarian should encourage them to explore reference sources independently. For instance, staff can try following posted guide sheets to learn how to use a reference CD-ROM. As always, they should report back to the librarian and discuss their experiences. In some cases, staff can point out flaws in the instructions and thereby help develop clearer guide sheets. Sometimes, students discover wonderful little facts or features in reference works, which they can share with the librarian and thus expand the resource's usefulness.

Student staff may concentrate on a reference area of personal interest to become a subject specialist. In one case, a student staff member had a passion for dogs, pit bulls in particular, and learned how to use a vast array of references in order to dig out more information about his interest. Not only is that student now contemplating making dog training and research his career, but the librarian polished her reference strategies and collection use through training this student.

If the school has a library club, then reference skills can be taught during each meeting. The librarian can introduce a new reference work, or, better yet, hand the resource to a student staff member ahead of time and have that person give the presentation at the meeting. Instruction can be keyed to timely issues—holidays or current events. Campaign time, for instance, offers a perfect opportunity to show how to use political references. Nationalistic struggles lend themselves well to atlas instruction. Centennials call for historical materials. And, again, student staff can bring up ideas for reference instructional content.

The underlying message is that reference skills do not exist in a vacuum, so shouldn't be approached that way. Librarians generally teach reference skills to classes within a meaningful context, such as a unit under current investigation. That same approach should be applied when teaching student staff the reference skills they need to help others in the library.

Techniques for conducting reference interviews

Objectives:

The student will conduct a reference interview with a peer, which will satisfy the peer's reference need.

Process:

The trainer conducts a sample interview with the student and then discusses the process. The trainer gives general guidelines for conducting reference interviews. The student practices interviewing the trainer; then the trainer observes and evaluates peer reference interviews.

Demonstration ideas:

- Have the student observe librarian-student reference interviews and then discuss the process with the librarian afterwards.
- Videotape actual reference interviews and discuss the process and strategies after viewing.
- Discuss past reference interviews that the student experienced, and critique them in terms of approach and results.

Student activities:

Give students a reference source and have them determine what kind of assignment or reference need could be satisfied using that source.
- Pose several opening lines for reference queries, and have the students carry out the reference interview.
- Have students create and do skits demonstrating effective and ineffective interviewing strategies.

Follow-up:

Link the reference interview with the collection, emphasizing the use of the resources in the entire library. Link the reference interview with research strategies, both offline and online. Link the reference interview with other forms of formal and informal instruction.

Evaluation:

Does the student
- Communicate clearly with the inquirer?
- Ask relevant and clear questions?

- Listen carefully?
- Interact with the inquirer in a friendly and respectful manner?
- Accurately determine the specific reference need?
- Offer relevant suggestions about useful sources that satisfy the reference need?

Reference Interview Checklist

- Identify the user: student, teacher, parent.
  Tip: the user probably doesn't know the library, doesn't know how to phrase the question, and doesn't know what to expect.

- Engage the user.
  Smile, be friendly and approachable. Acknowledge the user and make eye contact. The user is very sensitive to nonverbal behavior.
  Sample phrase: "Would you like me to help you?"

- Determine what information the user wants for a specific need. The user often doesn't know how to phrase the question. The user doesn't always want to share the real question. He or she may need an access tool, such as a catalog or index, rather than a specific book. Ask if the question is for school. If so, follow-up questions can deal with the specific assignment and teacher.
  Sample phrase: "What kind of help would you like?"

- Translate the question into library terms.
  Use a book of subject headings to identify key words. Use a variety of strategies or terms to locate relevant sources (e.g., space-astronomy-solar system-universe). Walk with the user to the part of the library where his probable subject is located, and use browsing techniques to get at the specific need.

- Determine what material is needed: the quantity, the depth and difficulty, and the type (pictorial, charts, statistics, narrative). Show the user a couple of potentially useful sources, and observe his or her response. Piling a bunch of books in a user's arms is usually overwhelming and inefficient.
  Sample phrase: "Why do you need the information?" or "What is the purpose of this search?"

- Determine whether the user needs additional guidance.
  The user may need help deciphering an index or reading a map legend.
  Sample phrase: "Let me know if you want additional help."

- Follow up on the interview.
  Your question may lead to another query or to a modification. Ask the user how well the research is going. This also shows that the library staff cares about the person and her or his needs.)
  Sample phrase: "Did you find what you wanted?"

Reference Interview: Query Quiz

When a library user asks for help, what information does that person really want? The inquirer may be reluctant to say or not know how to pose the question. Sometimes, the inquirer tries to guess what library terms or sources should be mentioned—and guesses wrong. While it is usually good to accept a person's statement at face value, a follow-up question or two can prevent frustration.

Decide which interpretation is the accurate one for each statement below.

1. Do you have any history books?
a) She wants to know if the library has history books.
b) She is looking for a copy of the school's world history textbook.
c) She wants to know the causes of the Cold War.

2. I need a bibliography on presidents.
a) He wants a bibliography on presidents.
b) He wants a biography of a U. S. President.
c) He wants a two-page chronology on the life of Sadat.

3. I need pictures of cats.
a) She wants pictures of cats.
b) She wants a photograph of a Siamese cat to copy for a painting.
c) She wants to cut pictures out of magazines for a collage of endangered tigers.

4. Where's the catalog?
a) He doesn't see the library card catalog, which is around the corner.
b) He can't find the card catalog because the library catalog is online.
c) He wants the school course catalog.

5. I want something on children.
a) She wants a book about children.
b) She wants diagrams about fetal development.
c) She wants a handbook on baby sitting.
d) She wants a chart comparing birth control methods.

If you picked "a" for any of these, you probably haven't finished your reference interview. You really can't second-guess what the inquirer wants.

Most reference interviews require follow-up questions. The easiest way to proceed is to ask the user to describe the kind of information he or she wants or why he or she wants it. You can also follow up later by asking the person if he or she found the information.

In the first question, for example, you would probably respond this way: "Yes, we have many history books. Are you looking for something in particular?" The inquirer would then give more details, such as "I need to read a book about the Middle Ages." At this point, you might walk the person to the 940.1 section and help her or him browse, and focus the inquiry even more. The inquirer will usually let you know if she or he is satisfied, either verbally or through body language (grab a volumn enthusiastically or shrug in disgust).

General research strategies

Objectives:	The student will use a variety of research strategies to locate information relevant to specific research needs.

Process: The trainer traces the research process, pointing out the underlying principles of research strategies. The trainer and student develop and apply specific research strategies to satisfy particular kinds of reference needs. The trainer critiques student research strategies.

Demonstration ideas:
- Videotape actual sessions where the librarian or user develops a research strategy. Critique the process afterwards.
- Create a set of index cards, each listing a research strategy step (e.g., use an encyclopedia, interview an expert in the field, find a statistical yearbook). Pose a research question, and have the student decide which cards to use.
- Have the student shadow the librarian's research strategies with other users, and discuss the process afterwards with the librarian.
- Create a guide sheet for reference sources that cover a specific subject.

Student activities: Provide students with the beginning and ending steps of a research strategy (i.e., the research question and the resultant sources), and have them list the intervening strategy steps.
- Have them develop a decision flow chart for research strategies.
- Give students a set of research topics, and have them develop a research strategy for each.
- Have students create a "pathfinder" (i.e., research strategy bibliography) for a specific subject.
- Have students create an "issues" or "aspects" fact sheet for a specific subject.

Follow-up: Link the reference interview and research strategy. Compare offline and online research strategies.

Evaluation: Does the student
- Accurately determine the kind of information needed?
- Plan a thorough research strategy?
- Modify the research strategy as added information is found?

Research Strategy Worksheet for Taking Notes

Purpose of Research:
    Possible reference sources:

Question or Thesis Statement:

Key Words:

Different Aspects of the Question:
    History?
    People?
    Location?
    Statistics?
    Literary?
    Legalities?
    Research studies?
    Possible reference sources:

Different Aspects of the Sources:
    Format?
    Language?
    Depth of coverage?
    How current?
    Possible reference sources:

Key Words Related to Each Aspect:
    Possible reference sources:

PLAN OF ACTION:
Get background information.
Clarify definitions.
Use access tools such as indexes.
Find in-depth information.
Find facts in specialized reference sources.
Find current facts in periodicals and databases.
Try alternative sources such as video, pamphlets, interviews.
Document your steps: key words, access tools, sources, links.
Review and revise your question and key words.
Alternate between general information and specific facts.
Evaluate citations listed in each source as a possible next rsource.
Re-examine your topic: Is there enough information? Too much?
Research related fields such as education or history.

Pathfinder Template

Topic:

General Strategies:
The basic approach to take when researching the topic

Key Terms:
The basic set of words and phrases associated with the topic

Overview Background
Usually an encyclopedia

Reference Tools:
DDC numbers and titles of relevant reference materials

Biographical References:

Periodicals:
Titles of relevant magazines and newspapers
May include specialized indexes

Subject DDC Numbers:
DDC numbers and associated specific subject related to topic

Sample Pathfinder to the U.S. Cabinet

General Strategies:
Choose a department of government and find out about the department and
how it works by looking at
   U. S. Government Manual
   Washington Information Directory
   Books on the individual departments
Find out about its current issues by looking at
   World News Digest
   Magazines (look under the index heading "United States. Dept. of...")
Note: Sometimes the same issue arises year to year, such as crop failures or
drug smuggling. Finding how government dealt with an issue in the past and
seeing the factors involved can help determine how the cabinet approaches it now.

Find out about cabinet members by looking at:
Current Biography, Who's Who in America
World News Digest
Magazines

Find out about a particular political issue by looking at books, magazines,
clippings *Then* overlay the department, cabinet member, and issue to find the
specific stance that a cabinet member would take.

Reference Tools on the Government:

310	almanacs
310	*Statistical Abstracts of the United States*
320.973	*Washington Information Directory*
320.973	*Vital Statistics on American Politics*
320.973	*Congress and the Nation*
353	*U. S. Government Manual*
353.03	*Guide to the Presidency*
Internet:	Government Web sites

Biographical References:

920	*Current Biography*
920.073	*Who's Who in America*

Magazines:
Congressional Digest
News magazines
Newspapers

Sample Subject DDC Numbers:

327	Foreign policy
330	Economics
333.7	Environment
353	U. S. Government
355	Military
635	Agriculture

Sample Guide Sheet on Subject-Specific Reference Sources

Language and Literature Sources:

1. Look up the word "dude" in a slang dictionary and in *Brewer's Dictionary of Phrase and Fable*. Write down your comparison of the entries. Using a thesaurus, write down a synonym and an antonym for "dude."

2. Write down where your first language, or an ancestor's first language, fits into the world's language tree.

3. What do the initials "ABC" stand for?

4. Write down your comparison of the entries on "Antigone" in *Ancient Writers* and *Harper's Classical Literature*.

5. Choose an American or British author.
   - Cite three reference sources containing information on the person, and write a unique fact found in each.
   - Find the title of a book by the author, and write a one-sentence summary of it using the *World Digest of Books*.
   - Find a character created by the author, and write a one-sentence description of him or her using the *Reader's Encyclopedia*.

Sample Issues Fact Sheet

Religious and Philosophical Sources

Directions: Write down a short note with the title and page of the source where you found following:

Map of Palestine (around the time of Jesus)
Muslim law
Taoist ethics
Explanation of a creation story
U.S. religion as an academic discipline
Number of Buddhists in your home (or ancestor's) country
Saint celebrated on your birthday
Religious significance of mistletoe
Picture of a Jewish shekel
Occurrences of the word "girl" in the Bible
New Age leaders in the U.S.
Picture of Angkor Wat
Ishtar
Theory of negative reinforcement
Epicurean philosophy
Cultural differences in perception
Controversy over euthanasia
Discussion of abortion ethics

The library catalog

Objectives:	The student will locate resources by using the catalog. The student will accurately interpet catalog record information. The student will distinguish among types of catalogs (if available).
Process:	The trainer shows the features of the library catalog, and explains catalog record information. The trainer demonstrates different ways to locate information by using the various features of the catalog. The student practices with the catalog to locate sources.

Demonstration ideas:

- Create a 9" x 12" reproduction of a catalog record. Laminate the card. Have the student label the parts of the record using a wipe-able marker.
- Create a 9" x 12" reproduction of a catalog record. Cut apart each piece of information (e.g., call number, author, tracings), and have the student put the card together.
- Together with the student, create a set of catalog cards based on a student's report or existing library resource.

Student activities:

Have the student
- Locate the entire catalog set for one book in a library card catalog.
- List information that can be found using a catalog, and compare it with a list of information that can be found using an index.
- Compare an online or CD-ROM catalog with a card catalog.

Follow-up: Review filing rules and the classification system. Link catalogs with other access tools.

Evaluation:

Can the student
- Correctly identify catalog record information?
- Locate sources using a catalog?
- Describe several ways to access a source?
- Accurately and thoroughly distinguish among types of catalogs?

Library Catalogs

Summary

- The catalog lists a library's sources.

- The main access point, known as the **main entry**, is usually the **author card** or entry.

- Each source has a set of entries: **author, title, subject**.

- Each entry gives information so you can decide if you want to use that source.

- The library catalog's entries are filed alphabetically, by first line.

- Library catalogs have different formats: **card, computer, microform**.

◀ Go Back | Help! | 🔳 Map | **Main Menu** | QUIT Continue ▶

Library Catalogs

Start looking for library material by using the library catalog.

The catalog lists all the books owned by a library, and often lists periodicals and resources in other formats.

The catalog also gives information about each resource so you can decide if you want to use that source.

The catalog does NOT list:
- individual articles in serials
- individual works within collections and anthologies
- all microform materials

◀ Go Back | Help! | 🔳 Map | **Main Menu** | QUIT Continue ▶

Library Catalogs

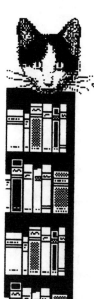

The library catalog offers many points of access to the collection:
- title
- author
- subject
- series (a continuing collection of volumes)
- call number (location code)

Computer tip:
Computerized catalogs often have additional access points, including key words.

◀ Go Back | Help! | Map | Main Menu | QUIT Continue ▶

Library Catalogs

The main access point, known as the **main entry**, is usually the **author card** or entry.
It gives the most complete information.

```
401.9
M       Moyne, John A.
             Understanding language: man or machine /
        John A. Moyne. – New York : Plenum Press, c1985.
             xvi, 357 p. : ill ; 24 cm.
             (Foundations of computer science)
             Includes index.
             ISBN 0-306-41970-X

             1. Psycholinguistics.  2. Linguistics–Data
        Processing.  I. Title.  II. Series.
        P37.M69      1985          401.9          85-12341
```

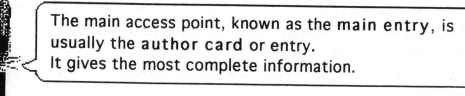

◀ Go Back | Help! | Map | Main Menu | QUIT Continue ▶

Library Catalogs

Each source has a set of cards, or entries, to help you find what you need.
Below is the SUBJECT card set for one title.

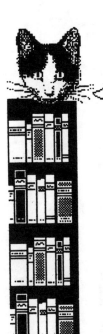

> Subject

```
P        PSYCHOLINGUISTICS
P        LINGUISTICS–DATA PROCESSING
37       Moyne, John A.
.M69        Understanding language: man or machine /
1985     John A. Moyne. – New York : Plenum Press, c1985.
            xvi, 357 p. : ill ; 24 cm.

            1. Psycholinguistics.  2. Linguistics–Data
         Processing.  I. Title.  II. Series.
         P27 M69    1985        401.9          85-12341
```

◁ Go Back | Help! | Map | **Main Menu** | QUIT Continue ▷

Library Catalogs

To find out which subject heading is used for a topic, first think of words and phrases that describe it.
Then look these terms up in the library's book of subject headings.

The library catalog also has cross-reference entries to the subject headings being used.

◁ Go Back | Help! | Map | **Main Menu** | QUIT Continue ▷

Indexes examined in terms of features and techniques for using them

Objectives: The student will locate a variety of sources by using indexes.

Process: Using a sample index, the trainer explains the generic features and use of an index. The trainer shows other indexes, and has the student compare them in terms of features and use. The student locates sources using the indexes.

Demonstration ideas:
- Photocopy guide sheets from indexes for student self-paced instruction.
- Enlarge or reconstruct an index entry, then cut apart each piece of information (e.g., article title, date, page number). Have the student put the pieces together.
- Trace the steps in constructing an index. Have the student watch a student yearbook being indexed.

Student activities: Have the student
- Research a topic using a variety of indexes, and compare the results.
- Develop a comparative chart of indexes, noting coverage, features, and use.
- Index a school publication, such as a newspaper.

Follow-up: Compare indexes, tables of contents, and library catalogs. Compare abstracts and indexes. Compare search engines and written indexes. Explain different index processes, such as KWIC (Key Word In Context) and KWOC (Key Word Out of Context).

Evaluation: Can the student
- Correctly identify the appropriate index to use for specific reference need?
- Locate sources by using indexes?

Indexes and Abstracts

Why use indexes?

There are two methods for finding articles on any topic.
You can either randomly look through a journal until you are lucky enough to find a relevant article, or you can use an index or an abstract.

Click on hands

What is an index?   A way of accessing articles - or books and reports - by subject

What is an abstract?   A summary of an article or other publication

◁ **Go Back** ‖ **Help!** ‖ 🔲 **Map** ▷   **Main Menu**   QUIT ‖ **Continue** ▷

Indexes and Abstracts

How do you use an index?

When you look for books you use the library catalog to look up an author or a subject. Use the same approach in a periodical index to find citations to specific articles.

There are different types of indexes:
General (e.g., *Reader's Guide to Periodical Literature*),
Subject (e.g., *Play Index*),
Specific Periodical (e.g., *National Geographic Society*),
Reviews (e.g., *Book Review Digest*).

Check with the librarian to find out how periodicals are arranged in each library.

◁ **Go Back** ‖ **Help!** ‖ 🔲 **Map** ▷   **Main Menu**   QUIT ‖ **Continue** ▷

Indexes and Abstracts

Sample Index

Look by each arrow to see what term refers to.

POLLITT, KATHA
Reading books, great or otherwise.
Harper's 283:34 D '92   ⇦ subject heading
POLLUTION   ⇦ entry / citation
See also
Acid rain
Oil pollution   ⇦ see reference
   Control   ⇦ subheading
Progress. P. V. Fossel *Country Journal*
  18:12-13 S/O '91
   International Aspects   ⇦ subheading subdivison
Earth alarm. I. Asimov. *World Monitor*
  4:58-60+ N '91
   Arkansas
The environmental morass in

◁ Go Back   **Main Menu**

Indexes and Abstracts

Examine the citation

Look at the labels to see what the parts of citation below are:

subject heading

see reference

article title

author

journal title

volume number
page numbers
date

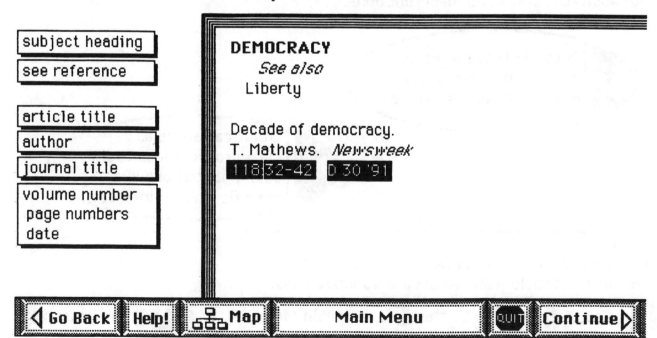

DEMOCRACY
See also
Liberty

Decade of democracy.
T. Mathews. *Newsweek*
118 32-42 D 30 '91

◁ Go Back   Help!   🖧 Map   **Main Menu**   QUIT   Continue ▷

Indexes and Abstracts

Abstracts

 While periodical indexes help you to locate references to articles...

 abstracts go a step further by briefly describing the contents of the article.

 This short "abstract" or summary usually contains the essential contents of the article.

 ◁ Go Back | Help! | Map | Main Menu | QUIT | Continue ▷

Indexes and Abstracts

Abstracts

An abstract serves two main functions:

 it can indicate whether it would be worthwhile to read the entire article

 and it can serve as a current awareness tool to scan publications in a specific area of interest.

Inside tip:
Abstracts may not always be accurate. It is best to consult the article itself to decide its usefulness.

◁ Go Back | Help! | Map | Main Menu | QUIT | Continue ▷

Training Library Student Staff

Indexes and Abstracts

How do you use an abstracts volume?

 Most abstracts will have a general subject and author index volume. Some abstracts will also have a listing specific to the field: in Biological Abstracts there is a genus species index.

 Use the index to find brief information about possible abstracts. Each entry includes the abstract number.

 The separate abstract section is usually arranged topically in abstract number order. Entries contain full bibliographic information, followed by the complete abstract.

◁ Go Back | Help! | 🖧 Map | Main Menu | QUIT | Continue ▷

Indexes and Abstracts

Look in the index for feasible citations

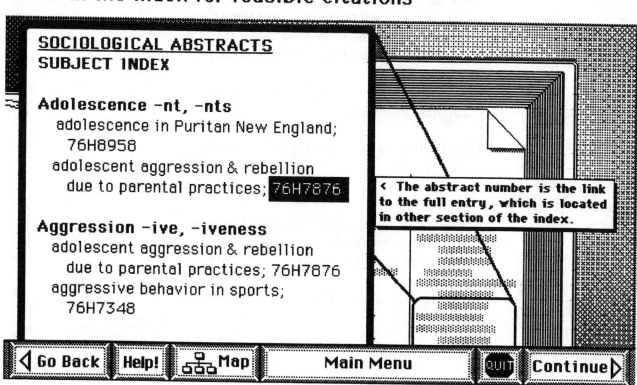

SOCIOLOGICAL ABSTRACTS
SUBJECT INDEX

Adolescence -nt, -nts
   adolescence in Puritan New England;
      76H8958
   adolescent aggression & rebellion
   due to parental practices; 76H7876

Aggression -ive, -iveness
   adolescent aggression & rebellion
      due to parental practices; 76H7876
   aggressive behavior in sports;
      76H7348

< The abstract number is the link to the full entry, which is located in other section of the index.

◁ Go Back | Help! | 🖧 Map | Main Menu | QUIT | Continue ▷

General and specialized dictionaries

Objectives: The student will find relevant definitions and other information by using a variety of dictionaries. The student will find specific facts and features, within a dictionary.

Process: Using a sample dictionary, the trainer explains the generic arrangement, features and use of a dictionary. The trainer shows other dictionaries, and has the student compare them in terms of features and use. The trainer points out the relative strengths of different dictionaries. The student locates definitions and specific facts amd features in dictionaries.

Demonstration ideas:
- Photocopy guide pages from dictionaries for students to use as self-paced lessons.
- Have the student explore a couple of dictionaries and create a list of the different kinds of information to be found in dictionaries.
- Use the analogy of anatomy and "dissect" a dictionary.

Student activities: Have the student
- Look up the same word in different dictionaries, and compare the results. This is particularly interesting if the student uses slang and etymological dictionaries as well.
- Research a family of words in a dictionary (e.g., biblio).
- Trace a word's origin back to the associated language dictionary.

Follow-up: Link dictionaries with other types of reference tools.

Evaluation: Does the student
- Identify the most useful dictionary, depending on the reference need?
- Find relevant definitions using a variety of dictionaries?
- Find specific facts and features using a variety of dictionaries?

Dictionary Comparison Chart

Title	Number of Volumes	Number of Pages	Average Entry Length	Special Features	Strengths

General and specialized encyclopedias

Objectives: The student will find relevant articles by using a variety of encyclopedias. The student will find specific facts and features within an encyclopedia.

Process: Using a sample encyclopedia, the trainer explains the generic features and use of an encyclopedia. The trainer shows other encyclopedias, and has the student compare them in terms of features and use. The trainer points out the relative strengths of different encyclopedias. The student locates articles and specific facts and features in encyclopedias.

Demonstation ideas: If training a number of students simultaneously, use one of these alternative methods:
- Different volumes of the same encyclopedia,
- The same lettered volume of different encyclopedia titles, or
- Several copies of the first volume of one encyclopedia (often available for less than a dollar at the local supermarket).
- Photocopy the encyclopedia's guidelines for use, and have the student do self-paced learning.
- Have an encyclopedia salesperson describe the features and use of an encyclopedia.
- Brainstorm with the student all the aspects of an encyclopedia, and together develop a chart comparing encyclopedias.
- Develop an encyclopedia scavenger hunt.

Student activities: Have the student
- Compare the same subject using a variety of encyclopedias.
- Locate a group of related articles, using the encyclopedia's index, article cross-references, and possible end notes of an article.
- Compare the print and CD-ROM versions of the same encyclopedia.
- Compare a general encyclopedia with a specialized encyclopedia.
- Play a trivia question game using encyclopedias to answer the questions.

Follow-up: Link encyclopedias with other types of reference tools. Describe how encyclopedias are developed and updated.

Evaluation: Does the student
- Identify the most useful encyclopedia, depending on the reference need?
- Find relevant articles using a variety of encyclopedias?
- Find specific facts and features using a variety of encyclopedias?

Encyclopedia Comparison Chart

Title	Number of Volumes	Average Number of Pages per Volume	Average Entry Length	Special Features	Strengths

General and specialized atlases

Objectives: The student will find relevant maps by using a variety of atlases. The student will find specific facts and features within an atlas. the student will interpret map information by correctly reading legends.

Process: Using a sample atlas, the trainer explains the generic features and use of an atlas. The trainer explains projections and legends. The trainer shows other atlases, and has the student compare them in terms of features and use. The trainer points out the relative strengths of different atlases. The student locates maps and specific facts and features in atlases. The student interprets map information.

Demonstration ideas:
- Have the student wrap tracing paper over globe and generate a map. Compare map projections.
- Photocopy a series of maps with legends. Separate the maps from the legends, and have the student combine them correctly.
- Take a computer atlas "tour."
- Together with the student, brainstorm possible information to be found in atlases. Locate the information in different types of atlases.
- Create an atlas scavenger hunt.

Student activities: Have the student
- Search the same geographical region in different maps and compare the results. Historical and thematic atlases enrich this activity.
- Trace the same geographic area through history using atlases.
- Compare two different geographic regions strictly from information found on maps.
- Create a map and associated legend.

Follow-up: Link atlases with gazetteers.

Evaluation: Can the student
- Identify the most useful atlas, depending on the reference need?
- Find relevant maps using a variety of atlases?
- Find specific facts and features using a variety of atlases?
- Correctly interpret map information by reading legends?

Atlas Comparison Chart

Title	Coverage	Types of Maps	Arrangement	Features	Strengths

Different sources of statistical information

Objectives: The student will locate statistical information using a variety of statistical sources. The student will correctly interpret statistical information. The student will describe different types of statistical resources.

Process: The trainer defines and describes statistical information. The trainer shows different types of resources that contain statistical information. The trainer explains how to interpret statistical information. The student practices skills in locating and interpreting statistical information.

Demonstration ideas:
- Together with the student, brainstorm types of statistical information that students might want to find. Locate resources that have the needed information.
- Together with the student, choose a subject or geographic area. Locate as many relevant statistical sources as possible.
- Use access tools to locate statistical sources.
- Take representative statistical charts and brainstorm with the student about different conclusions that can be drawn from the figures.
- Take sample reference tools, such as atlases and encyclopedias, and locate statistical information in them.

Student activities: Have the student
- Choose a subject or geographic area
- Transform one form of statistical information (e.g., table) into another form (e.g., bar graph).
- Interpret and draw conclusions from, several statistical charts.

Follow-up: Explain how statistical information can be misleading. Explain how to evaluate the authoritativeness of statistical information.

Evaluation: Can the student
- Choose the best statistical source for a specific reference?
- Locate statistical information within a source?
- Accurately interpret statistical information?
- Identify and compare different statistical sources?

Statistics

Numerical facts or data which have been collected, classified, analyzed or interpreted are called statistics.

Statistics can be divided into two basic types:

 Economic/Social

 Scientific/Technical

In application, statistics refers to numbers and numerical facts. People use these numbers to see trends and make decisions.

Statistics is a field of science which uses mathematical methods to analyze numerical data.

◀ Go Back | Help! | Map | Main Menu | QUIT | Continue ▶

Statistics

Some example statistics include:

- ● **population or demographic statistics**
  How many people live in California?
  What percentage of women smoke?

- ● **industry statistics**
  How many cars were manufactured last year?
  How many board feet of lumber are used in the U. S. yearly?

- ● **ranking statistics**
  What's the healthiest city in the U. S.?
  What country has the highest Gross National Product?

- ● **opinion statistics**
  Do Europeans view themselves as politically left or right?
  What do Americans think about nuclear disarmament?

◀ Go Back | Help! | Map | Main Menu | QUIT | Continue ▶

Statistics

Search in the library's catalog under the particular subject you are interested in, adding the words"statistics" after the subject.

Once you locate the source, use its **index** to find the specific topic or category.

LOCATING SOURCES

For example:
If you search under the topic
"Latin America--Statistics"

You will most likely find
Statistical Abstract of Latin America

◁ **Go Back**

Statistics

Types of statistical sources include:

general dictionaries and compendiums

almanacs or annuals

census reports and other government sources

national/state yearbooks and statistical annuals

periodicals

statistics of a particular subject: farming, commerce

trade and professional association reports

◁ **Go Back** | **Help!** | 🔲 **Map** | **Main Menu** | QUIT | **Continue** ▷

Sources of biographical information

Objectives:

The student will correctly identify biographical sources. The student will locate biographical sources. The student will determine the specific source most likely to satisfy a biographical reference need.

Process:

Using a general biographical reference source, the trainer explains the generic features of biographical material and stratagies to locate relevant sources. The trainer shows other biographical sources and has the student compare them in terms of type and features. The trainer points out the relative strengths of different sources. The student locates biographies and specific facts and features in different sources.

Demonstration ideas:

- Together with the student, brainstorm a list of famous people, and locate information on them in different biographical sources.
- Different occupations or attributes (e.g., gender, ethnicity), and locate collective biographies and directories for each. Note specialized indexes in some biographical sources, such as *Current Biography.*
- Starting with a general biography, such as the *World Encyclopedia of Biography*, trace biographical sources cited in an article to its associated materials. A source "web" may be generated.

Student activities:

- Use access tools (e.g., catalog, indexes) to locate biographical information.
- Have the student use a variety of biographical sources to find information on a particular person, and compare the findings.
- Have the student create a list with the following dichotomous categories:
Individual or Collective
International or National
Contemporary or Retrospective/Historical
General or Subject-specific
- Have the student list biographical source titles, checking off the options for each. Have the student analyze the findings. A possible table format follows.

Title	Indiv/Col	Intl/Natl	Cont/Retro	Gen/Subj

Follow-up: Link biographic references with collective and
individual biographics.

Evaluation: Can the student
- Identify the most useful biographical source?

Internet uses and protocols

Objectives:

The student will explain and use the different functions of the Internet accurately and efficiently. The student will locate relevant information using the Internet.

Process:

The trainer describes the Internet.
- The trainer demonstrates and explains the entire process: log on, search strategy, file location, retrieval, download, logoff.
- The trainer shows some useful sites and sources.
- The trainer shows other "gateway" services such as e-mail and electronic bulletin boards.
- Student then tries each step, with the trainer coaching.

Demonstration ideas:

- Start with interesting sites and addresses and work backwards to demonstrate how the Internet functions.
- Have students act out parts of the Internet.
- Have the student self-teach using a videotape on Internet operations.
- Use WebWhacker (software program that downloads and "captures" Internet files and allows one to simulate an online Internet session) to teach Internet skills offline.

Student activities:

Have students
- Try different search engines to find the same information; have them analyze their results.
- Create their own WebWhacker instructional guide.
- Locate valuable sitesand addresses, and note them on index cards.

Follow-up:

Discuss remote databases and other telecommunication providers and gateways. Discuss the ethical use of the Internet. Discuss the need to evaluate sources. Link the Internet to research strategies.

Evaluation:

Does the student
- Successfully log on, use a search engine, locate and retrieve relevant information, download it, and log off?
- Locate information by referring to printed URLs (Uniform Resources Locators)?
- Display responsible and ethical Internet behavior?

Netscape Guidesheet

Connect!
Make sure you have a way to connect to an Internet provider, either by modem or highspeed line.

Start Netscape:
Locate and double-click on the Netscape icon. It opens to the home page. Scroll down the screen to read the information.

Link to a site:
Links are "hot text" that connect you to another page. You access the page you want by clicking on the different-colored or *underlined* text.

Use an address:
If you know the address to a location or site you want, you can type it in. (It's sometimes called a URL: Uniform Resource Locator.)

With Netscape, click the "Open" button. A dialogue box will pop up for you to type in the complete address.

How do you translate a URL?

http://Calacademy.org./~library/gbalc.html translated is: http:// is the protocol (e.g., hypertext transfer protocol)
Calacademy is the host computer
.org is the type of system (e.g., organization)
~library is the directory where the information is stored
gbalc.html is the Web page or file (html means hypertext mark-up language)

Search
Click on the "Net Search" button to activate a search engine. Each search engine is a program that looks for documents that have the topic you're looking for. Common search engines include: WebCrawler, Lycos, Magellan, and InfoSeek. Some search engines allow Boolean strategies. Use "Net Search" for unambiguous or multifaceted topics, such as "mononucleosis" or "Chinese filmmakers."

Click on the "Net Directory" button to activate a series of topical menus. By clicking on a topic link, you can narrow a broad topic down to a highly focused one. Use "Net Directory" when when you want to narrow down the kind of databases to be searched, such as "Mars" when you want just the planet and not the candy bar.

Bookmark
Want to go back to a particularly useful site later? Find Bookmark, and click on it. Drag the mouse down to "Add Bookmark." This stays on the system; you can even export the Bookmark onto a floppy disk to take elsewhere. (On other Internet browsers, "Bookmark" may be called "Favorites.")

Quit
Go to File, and drag the mouse down to "Quit." Sometimes the term used is "Exit."

Other Library Services

Each library has its own custom services that help define it. Depending on its mission, the library may offer regular events, discussion groups, production facilities, and fund raisers. In most cases, library student staff can participate in planning and managing these services. Not only do students like the status associated with these services, but for those occasional special programs, student staff who do not normally have time to engage in ongoing projects enjoy helping out on one-time projects.

Because each service is custom-designed to fill a need, care must be given to matching the service with the staff member. If the service is ongoing, the librarian can include it on the application form. If, however, the service is one-time only, then the librarian needs to approach staff at the project's planning time. Sometimes recruitment can be as easy as announcing an upcoming event at a library club and asking for student volunteers. At other times, the librarian may solicit the help of students who may be interested and skilled in the specific project.

In the ideal situation, student staff can initiate and plan special programs and services. If they come up with the idea, they have more ownership in its outcome, and will usually work harder to make it succeed. In those cases, the librarian can act as a facilitator rather than a director making sure that the staff have the information, access, and support needed to accomplish the project or service. If student staff are not skilled in planning, the librarian can help them develop those necessary skills, adding to the students' educational experience.

In any case, library services should be well known and supported by library student staff because they not only help implement those services but tell others about them and thus strengthen the library's image and impact.

Suggestions and planning guides for programs and events

Objectives:	The student will help implement library programs and events.
Process:	The trainer explains the program or event: its goals and objectives, its features, and its planning components. The trainer explains the process that students need to learn in order to help carry out the program or event. The trainer guides the students in their work.

Demonstration ideas:

- Share the documentation or a video from a similar program or event with the student. Ask students how they want to participate, and teach the specific associated tasks.
- Together with students, brainstorm possible programs and events. Develop a plan and train the students in those tasks that they want to work on.
- Have students visit another site with a potential program or event. Develop a plan with them to replicate the project in-house.

Student activities:

Have the student
- Create a planning flow chart or time line.
- Recruit others to help plan and carry out the project.
- Work with a co-sponsor to plan or carry out the project.

Follow-up:

Show how the program or event implements the library's mission. Link the program or event with other library services.

Evaluation:

Do the students
- Understand the program and event sufficiently?
- Plan effectively?
- Implement their parts of the plan effectively (on time, thoroughly, competently, responsibly)?
- Work well with others?

Program Planning Checklist

Objectives:
Content:
Potential participants:
Planners:
Funding sources:
Publicity:
Registration (and fees):
Co-sponsorship:
Date and time (including length):
Format (presentation, panel discussion, skit):
Site:
Site arrangement (theater, discussion tables, circled chairs):
Materials needed (equipment, handouts, food, furniture):
People needed (MC, speakers, helpers):
Method of evaluation:

One week before the event, make sure the following are in order:
- Responsible people: speakers, helpers, guides
- Supplies: paper, writing tools, stands, tape, food
- Equipment and back-up supplies (e.g., bulbs)
- Resources: Audiovisual sources, displays, handbouts, forms, signs

On the day of the event, make sure the following are taken care of:
- Placing signs
- Registration
- Runners
- Hosts and hostesses
- Parking
- Guides
- Handouts and distribution
- Equipment set-up
- Clean-up

Follow-up:
- Write thank-you notes
- Return all equipment and resources
- Turn in expense receipts and other invoices
- Gather and analyze evaluations

Program and Event Ideas

Readings: poetry, plays, novels, student work

Career exploration: interview skills, resume preparation, guidance counseling, community employers, money management

Social issues: panelists, videotapes, reporters, lobbyists, voting opportunities

Curriculum-related topics: rain forests, elections, genetics, AIDS, cultures, fractals, mime, fitness, writing, technology, Renaissance

Celebrations: holidays, special months (women's history, Black heritage)

Collections: books, pictures, memorabilia

Publishing: publishers, how-to workshops, publishing agents, writers

Media: cartoonists, broadcasters, animators, multimedia producers, filmmakers, musicians, actors, dancers

Personal interests: fashion and clothing, organizing skills, dating hints, car mechanics, astrology

Hobbies: calligraphy, wind surfing, race car driving, magic, travel, chess

Contest Ideas and Guidelines

Planning Considerations:

Budget far in advance.

Determine the objective.

Develop clear, simple rules for playing and winning.

Determine the time frame: Keep it short.

Aim for wide participation; make it easy to compete.

Get all supplies needed; look for co-sponsorship. Get prizes donated.

Get the word out!

Contest Inspirations:
- Crosswords or word searches
- Relays: pass the book, find the answer
- Research scavenger hunt
- Guess the number of books, magazines, checkouts
- Solve literary mysteries
- Book jacket design competition
- Library logo competition
- Literary costume competition
- Identifying quotations
- Book battles

Reader's advisory activities

Objectives: The student will identify a variety of reader's advisory activities. The student will carry out a reader's advisory activity.

Process: The trainer describes a reader's advisory activity: its goals and objectives, its features, and its planning components. The trainer explains the process that the student needs to learn in order to help carry out the program or event. The trainer explains other reader's advisory activities. The student chooses one activity to carry out, and the trainer guides the student in their work.

Demonstration ideas:
- Discuss with the student how teens choose reading material—books and magazines. Discuss what makes a good "read." Using those criteria, show the student review guidelines and sample reviews.
- Use a marketing or advertising model to explain how reading can be promoted. Brainstorm with the student possible advisory ideas.
- Share "best" lists, core collection books, and other reviewed or annotated bibliographies. Brainstorm with the student about ways to use these reference tools.

Student activities: Have the student
- Create a Top Ten reading list.
- Create reading posters with suggested titles.
- Create a display to encourage reading.
- Write reviews for the school newspaper or bulletin board.

Follow-up: Link reader's advisory with collection development. Link reader's advisory with public relations. Discuss how reader's advisory can approach bibliotherapy.

Evaluation: Can the student
- Identify a variety of reader's advisory activities?
- Advise peers and encourage reading to the peers' satisfaction?
- Carry out reader's advisory activities responsibly and competently?

Review Guidelines

Writing Structure:
Heading: Full citation: title, author, publisher, date, length

Paragraph 1: **Briefly summarize the book or product.** Grab the reader's attention with the first sentence. What is the intent of the author? Does he or she succeed?

Paragraph 2: **Analyze the content.**
- Who is the intended audience?
- What is the scope?
- How accurate and believable is the writing?
- If it's fiction, how well are the characters and plot developed?
- How well is it organized?
- How original and creative is it? Is the format effective? Is there a diversity of personal backgrounds and perspectives?
- How does it compare with similar books or products?

Paragraph 3: **Evaluate the technical and physical aspects.**
- Is it durable?
- Is it easy to view?
- Is the text legible?
- Is the color accurate?
- If sound or motion is included, is it appropriate and competently done?

Paragraph 4: **Make final conclusions.** Would you recommend it? Why?

Sign it: Reviewed by YOU!

Considerations to Include When Reviewing Technology:
Hardware requirements
Ease of installation
Special features

Alternative Formats:
Create a mock book jacket.
- Illustrate the front cover. Include the title and author.
- On the front inside flap, write paragraphs one and two.
- On the back inside flap, write something about the author. Include a picture if you want.
- On the back cover, write excerpts (i.e., enticing passages) from the book or write quotes from people who have enjoyed the book.

Create a poster!
- Create one compelling graphic or illustration as the focal point.
- In large letters, write the title and author.
- Write one paragraph that will entice someone to read the book. Use "sound bites!"
- You can make the poster look like a movie poster, with the cast of major characters written on the bottom portion of the poster.

Where To Place Reviews:
- Inside similar books
- In bookmarks
- At the ends of book shelves and ranges
- On bulletin boards and walls
- On easel signs
- On mobiles
- In teachers' mailboxes
- On placemats
- In newspapers and newsletters
- On Web pages

Displays To Encourage Reading

Basic Principles:
- One theme or message
- One unifying graphic
- A large, legible title
- Lettering that harmonizes (one or two fonts, sizes, and colors)
- Background appropriate to the theme (in color, design, shape)
- Asthetically pleasing in form, line, shape, value, texture, color, and use of space

Display Ideas:
- Holidays and seasons
- Famous people, places, events
- Costumes as backgrounds to display historic or literary books props: umbrellas for rainy-day books, portable loom for craft books, sports equipment, shells for nature or beachside reading
- Magazine covers as thematic background
- Student artwork as graphic theme
- Masks for plays or cultural works
- Models: transportation, figures, houses, animals, landscapes tracks: shoes, feet, animal tracks, roads, railways, trail signs
- Symbols: traffic signs, logos, religious, trademarks, light bulb for ideas
- Game boards and pieces; crossword puzzles; riddles and jokes

Copy ideas from magazines and posters!

Booktalking Techniques

Objectives: The student will create a booktalk. The student will memorize and booktalk at least three books to one or more persons.

Process: The trainer demonstrates a booktalk and explains the purpose and features of booktalks. The trainer shares written examples of booktalks. The trainer helps the student develop a booktalk. The trainer gives tips on giving booktalks. The trainer critiques student booktalks.

Demonstration ideas:
- Watch a videotape of booktalkers.
- Videotape student booktalks, and then critique them.
- Watch television programs that show book discussions.
- Attend booktalking sessions done by librarians, teachers, or book dealers.

Student activities: Have the student
- Adapt book jacket "blurbs" into booktalks.
- Find enticing book passages, and adapt them into booktalks.
- Create book"talks" for *BookWhiz* or *BookBrain* software programs.

Follow-up: Compare booktalks with storytelling, jacket "blurbs," reviews, and annotated bibliographies. Discuss the role of booktalking in relation to reader's advising.

Evaluation: Can the student
- Create a booktalk that accurately represents the book and engages the listener?
- Memorize a booktalk and present it accurately?
- Orally present a booktalk articulately and enthusiastically?

Booktalking the Curriculum

Books play an important role in education because they stimulate the imagination and the mind. Each type of book has its advantages and can be used in different ways.

Informational books give different perspectives about the subjects taught in school. They can cover topics in greater depth than can be handled in class time, and are available at different reading levels. Here are some ways to introduce these factual accounts:

- Pick out "trivia" facts in a fun question-and-answer session.
- Play "Twenty Questions" about a topic, giving clues from the book as the game progresses.
- Start a discussion with a "What if...," such as "What if there were no bridges," and introduce a book around the consequences.
- Enlarge illustrations from informational books, modify them as needed, and make overhead transparencies to booktalk with.
- "Spin" the book into a mystery format, and reveal the solution through booktalking; this is particularly good for books about inventions and discoveries.

Biographies make learning come alive; they create a personal dimension. Biographies also show how each individual can make a difference. Biographies are often dramatic stories, as well, and appeal to the reader's emotions. Here are ways to breathe life into biographies:

- Dress up as the character, and speak of first-hand experiences.
- With another student, prepare a "live" interview with the character.
- Dramatize one incident in the character's life.
- Hold up pictures of famous people for students to identify, and present mini-booktalks about each one or the group.
- Make a videotape or slide show about a character.

Historical novels provide insights about the human condition under different situations. Students identify with the protagonist, imagining themselves in the same era. Fiction transcends specific data to give a more three-dimensional perspective of the world. And students are impressed when they find out how much research fiction writers have to do in order to write a credible tale. Here are some strategies for sharing:

- Ask students what they would do in a particular situation, and then tell how the fictional character acted.
- Have student visualize being a particular character or being in a particular place in time, and then lead them through the story.
- Give several short booktalks about contemporaneous characters of the same historical period but in different countries.
- Focusing on one geographical area, such as France, give a fictional time line booktalk.
- Show slides or pictures of a historical period to accompany booktalks.

Poetry is an underutilized form, especially in booktalks. Yet poems can express the most profound details and insights about life. In addition, students respond to poetic rhythm and pithiness. Some students may be surprised to discover the breadth of subjects that poetry treats: mathematics, sports, transportation, and astronomy, to name a few. A good start when booktalking poetry is to consult *Granger's Guide to Poetry* or other poetry indexes by subject.

- Intersperse poems between other booktalks.
- Use poetry as an introductory or ending piece of a booktalk program.
- Include humorous poetry for comic relief.
- Treat a broad subject, such as war, through dramatic poetry readings.
- Coordinate poems with related artwork.

Further reading:

Caroline Feller Bauer. *Caroline Feller Bauer's New Handbook for Storytellers*. American Library Association, 1993.

Joni Bodart. *Booktalk, Booktalker, New Booktalker* and her other related titles produced by various publishers.

Storytelling techniques

Objectives: The student will work on telling a story. The student will memorize and tell at least two stories to an audience.

Process: The trainer tells a story and explains the purpose and features of storytelling. The trainer shares different techniques in storytelling. The trainer helps the student learn a story to tell. The trainer critiques student storytelling.

Demonstration ideas:
- Watch a videotape of storytellers.
- Videotape student storytellers, and then critique them.
- Watch television programs that show storytelling, such as *Reading Rainbow*.
- Attend storytelling sessions done by librarians, teachers, or professional storytellers.
- Collect "props" and tell stories using them.

Student activities: Have the students
- Use pictures to tell stories.
- Use puppets to tell stories.
- Create storytelling audiotapes.

Follow-up: Compare storytelling with reading from a book. Discuss the role of storytelling in relation to reader's advising.

Evaluation: Can the student
- Choose an appropriate story to tell?
- Memorize a story and "repeat" it accurately?
- Tell a story articulately and engagingly?

Guidelines for Telling a Story

1. Choose a story that you love—and would love to share.

2. Decide if that story would make good booktalking material. It should have:
   - Active and engaging language
   - Interesting characters that listeners can identify easily
   - A strong plot that is easily followed
   - An episode or session that can be shared in less than 10 minutes (for beginner booktalkers)

3. Read the story several times, preferably aloud. You can record it on an audiotape, and listen to your delivery. Time it.

4. *Think* about the story.
   - What does it mean to you?
   - Why is it special?
   - What kind of feeling does it evoke?
   - How can you help make it come alive?

5. Write down the story in your own handwriting.

6. Put the story away for a day.

7. Without looking at the story, try writing or drawing the key incidents or scenes in sequence.

8. Using the story as support, think of ways to remember the details. Make an index card for each scene. Create a mental picture of the story ("the movie in your head"). Memorize key phrases, such as a repeating rhyme or a turning point.

9. "Test-drive" the story by telling it aloud to someone or something: a willing friend, a stuffed toy, a full-length mirror. Check your voice, your body language and gestures, your anxiety level. Make eye contact.

10. Present your story! It gets easier each time you do it.

Techniques for conducting various kinds of discussion groups

Objectives: The student will identify different types of discussion groups. The student will outline the steps in developing and leading a discussion group. The student will help plan or lead a discussion group.

Process: The trainer explains the features and benefits of discussion groups. The trainer describes different types of discussion groups. The trainer outlines the steps in developing and leading a discussion group. The student helps plan or lead a discussion group.

Demonstration ideas:
- Attend an ongoing discussion group.
- Watch a television show where books, movies, music, or technology are discussed. Analyze the discussion steps and techniques.
- Discuss group dynamics and how they affect discussion groups.

Student activities:
- Develop a discussion group flow chart plan.
- Choose books, films, or computer programs to discuss.
- Brainstorm good questions to ask during a group discussion.

Follow-up: Compare reviews and discussion groups. Compare library discussion groups with classroom discussions.

Evaluation: Can the student
- Plan a discussion group in complete detail?
- Choose appropriate material to discuss?
- Elicit active and cogent participation when leading a discussion group session?

Steps in Developing a Discussion Group

1. Develop a general idea for a discussion group: science fiction writing or movies, mystery stories, teen novels, poetry, classic movies, non-Western literature, comics, historical romances, jazz compositions, or video games.

2. Determine outcomes or objectives for the group: To get tips on playing games, to understand complex stories, to discover other cultures, to socialize with people who have like interests, to learn more about the topic, to have friends to go to the movies with, to improve artistic skills.

3. Announce the idea: tell friends, put up posters, have a booth at a club sign-up event.

4. Conduct a planning meeting with potential participants:
   - Decide on a couple of books or films to start the group going and plan how to choose future selections.
   - Decide who will lead the discussion. (It's more fun to rotate the discussion leader.)
   - Determine place (hopefully, the library) time, frequency, length of discussion, food.
   - Make sure everyone has a chance to read or view the selection ahead of time. (If there's enough time during the discussion group meeting, the members can actually view or listen to the selection and talk about it immediately thereafter (e.g., poem, video, recording, computer program).

5. Lead the discussion. Here are some tips:
   - Come prepared. Think of some good discussion questions or comments ahead of time.
   - Start on time, and stop on time.
   - Start with a controversial or key point. It may be a crucial passage, a dilemma that a character has to face, or a point that you disagree with.
   - Ask open-ended questions. "What if..."s elicit good responses.
   - Encourage everyone to participate. Keep the group on task.
   - Maintain a pleasant atmosphere; make sure everyone is enjoying the discussion. Note that controversy is okay if it helps bring new perspectives and is discussed in a nonthreatening manner.

6. Keep the group going:
   - Develop an expectation of regular attendance and preparedness to discuss.
   - Announce upcoming meetings so everyone knows and can plan ahead.
   - If problems arise, solve them quickly so they don't fester and bog down the group.

Tutoring techniques

Objectives:
The student will use tutoring techniques that facilitate the learner's progress in information literacy.

Process:
The trainer will demonstrate effective tutoring techniques. The trainer will help the student determine the critical features of effective tutoring. The trainer will coach the student as he or she practices tutoring others.

Demonstration ideas:
- Videotape effective tutoring practices and analyze the process.
- Have a professional tutor demonstrate effective techniques and practices.
- Discuss with the student past experiences in being tutored or coached.
- Develop a list of effective and ineffective techniques.

Student activities:
Have the student
- Train another library staff member.
- Critique another person's tutoring techniques.
- Interview tutors and learners in terms of effective techniques.
- Write directions for a library task.

Follow-up:
Discuss the relationship of tutoring to large-group discussion. Compare tutoring with self-guided instruction. Discuss the significance of interpersonal skills relative to successful tutoring.

Evaluation:
Does the student
- Communicate articulately with the trainee?
- Explain the skill or process clearly and accurately?
- Practice good interpersonal skills?
- Does the trainee learn from the tutor well enough to accomplish the task or apply the concept effectively?

Tips on Becoming an Effective Library Tutor

Basic Steps:
1. Clarify what the person wants to learn.
2. Agree on what you will teach.
3. Agree on the length of time.
4. Find an appropriate place to tutor.
5. Have all materials and resources available.
6. Find out what the person already knows.
7. Explain one concept at a time. Define all unknown terms.
8. Demonstrate or model the skill.
9. Walk through the process one step at a time. Check to make sure the person understands before continuing to the next step.
10. Have the person explain the concept. Correct as needed.
11. Have the person go through the process. Correct as needed.
12. Have the person practice the skill, being able to ask for help as needed.
13. Ask the person if he or she needs any more help. Repeat steps as needed.
14. Thank the person and leave him or her to work independently.

General Hints:
- Be professional: Be friendly, respectful, and helpful.
- Communicate effectively: Be clear and articulate, be heard, be thorough.
- Listen attentively and respond appropriately.
- Be patient and keep a sense of humor.

Establishing a Tutoring Program

1. Train a number of library student staff as tutors. Certify them for specific areas of expertise: circulation routines, magazine index use, Internet searching, desktop publishing, videotaping. A certified tutor card made from a half index card may be created for each person.

2. Develop a database of library student staff tutors. Using the following fields:

Name	Specialties	Availability	Sign-up

The database can be sorted by specialty and availability.

3. Post the database. Faculty and students can sign up for tutoring, or simply ask the tutor if she or he is available for quick help. If the posted list is laminated, scheduling can be done with a wipeable marker each day or week.

4. Encourage trainees to evaluate their tutors.

5. Provide opportunities for tutors to improve their skills.

6. Recognize good work.

Production planning principles

Objectives:

The student will identify and follow the planning steps involved in producing a product for a teacher. The student will apply basic artistic and interface design principles when creating communication aids. The student will produce a product that is of acceptable quality to the teacher.

Process:

The trainer shares several examples of well-executed and poorly-executed products. The trainer explains and demonstrates the steps involved in planning and producing a product for a teacher. The trainer coaches the students as they follow the steps for planning and producing a product for a teacher.

Demonstration ideas:

• Make a videotape that traces the planning and production steps in creating a product for a teacher.
• Together with the student, determine the critical features of a well-planned and executed product. Practice the techniques needed to create a high-quality product.
• Ask teachers how they develop teaching aids.

Student activities:

Have the student
• Create a product planning flow chart.
• Modify an existing product, getting input for changes from another person (preferably an adult).
• Develop a product plan and carry it out.

Follow-up:

Link production principles to equipment use. Link production principles to communications principles. Link planning skills to tutoring techniques.

Evaluation:

Does the student
• Work effectively with the teacher to plan and create an acceptable product?
• Accurately translate the teacher's idea into an acceptable format that communicates the concepts effectively?
• Artistic and design principles effectively when creating the product?
• Work responsibly and efficiently?

Production Planning Guide

To the Teacher:
Use this form to plan a teaching aid or product. Our library staff will work
with you to create a satisfactory result. Use additional sheets as needed to
detail the desired product.

Teacher:
Staff Assigned:
Time Frame:

Product:
Objective:
Use:
Audience:
Content:
Format:
Length:

Design Considerations:
Theme (unifying look):
Graphics:
Type:
Text:
Color schemes (if there's a preference):
Sound or motion, if any:
Interactive features, if any:
Layout:
Sequencing/branching:

Please include any documentation that would help in creating the product
(e.g., text, images, mock-ups, sources).

Interface Design Principles

<u>KISS = Keep it simple, staff!</u>

Be consistent.
Have a unifying theme. The images, type fonts, wording should reinforce each other. For example, a poster advertising a melodrama could have a Western theme communicated through a dancehall stage border, old-time "carved" looking typeface, and exaggerated melodramatic text.
Maintain a consistent tone, be it serious or humorous.
Have a consistent appearance. Pages or screens should look as though they belong together. Use only one or two type fonts and sizes. Use the same artistic style, be it line drawings or high-contrast photography. Use a style sheet to follow conventions (e.g., bibliographic citation style or **highlighting** conventions).

Be clear.
Use plain language that the user can understand.
If symbols are used, especially as visual cues, make sure the user understands them (e.g., return arrow, home icon, pointer finger).
If the concept or process is sequential, number the steps.
If the user can make choices, explain how to choose. If appropriate, tell the result of the choice ahead of time (e.g.., "If you want to open the door, click on the A button. If you want to open the window, click on the B button.")
Make the product look organized so the user doesn't get confused or disoriented.
Don't have so many "bells and whistles" that the user overlooks the content and message.
Be concise.

Be engaging!
Use color, images, sound, or motion to attract the user.
Build in options and choices so the user has some control. Perhaps the user can skip the review. Perhaps the user can choose one of several characters to follow in a story.
Provide feedback. For instance, if a response is called for, tell the user if the response is correct or not; give the correct answer or provide further hints and let the user try again.
Make it enjoyable.

Pilot-Test the Product Before It's Done!
Does it work? If not, modify it now!

Fund-raising ideas and plans

Objectives:
The student will identify possible fund-raising ideas. The student will identify and follow steps to plan and implement fund-raising activities. The student will play a significant role in a fund-raising activity.

Process:
The trainer will show examples of fund raisers. The trainer explains the planning steps involved in fund raising. The trainer helps the student plan a fund raiser.

Demonstration ideas:
• Attend other fund raisers, and analyze their plans and implementation.
• Share fund raiser documents and analyze them for effect and planning usefulness.
• Discuss and critique fund raisers that the student attended.

Student activities:
Have the student
• Brainstorm fund raising ideas.
• Develop a plan for a fund-raising activity.
• Volunteer to help at another fund raiser, and evaluate its plan and implementation.

Follow-up:
Link fund raisers to other library programs and events. Discuss money management issues. Show how the budget is affected by fund raisers.

Evaluation:
Can the student
• Identify possible fund-raising activities?
• Develop a fund-raising plan?
• Follow a fund-raising plan efficiently?
• Does the student act responsibly and competently during the fund-raising plan and implementation?

Fund-Raising Plan Guidelines

Planning Considerations:
Get permission from the librarian and principal.
Get sponsorship and major support: Ask the right people.
Get the resources: space, human, material.
Determine the time frame: one-shot, annual, period, ongoing.
Do the publicity. Use a variety of media (fliers, radio, posters) and a variety of distribution means (newspapers, parent newsletters, student announcements).

Potential Sponsors:
Other school entities
Parents
Civic groups
Community members
Other libraries
Other schools
Local businesses
Grant-giving institutions

Fund-Raising Ideas:
Book sale (new or used books)
Video showing
Celebrity books or autograph auction
Read-a-thon
Computer-customized note cards and letterheads
Hand-lettered products
Bookmarks
Library publications
Library logo products (bags, T-shirts)
Library-produced videotapes
Computer services on demand
Computer training or tutoring on demand
Booktalking or storytelling on demand
Library-produced publications, Web pages

Communications

Communication is at the heart of the library—minds communicating with minds through books, magazines, and other sources. Library instruction is another manifestation of communication—helping others learn how to access these sources, physically and intellectually, as well as to use the ideas they find. Some library services and programs focus on communication: readers' advisory, booktalking and storytelling, productions.

Yet for all the communication that occurs in the library, communication *about* the library is sometimes neglected. And if no one knows about the library, all that communication *within* the library will be underused and undervalued. Remember, a message isn't really communicated until it is received *and responded to*.

What are some of those messages?

- That the library offers great services and programs,
- That the library has great adult and student staff,
- That the library keeps in touch with its community and supports it,
- That the library responds to user needs,
- That the library has certain needs, and
- That the library communicates!

Fortunately, library student staff can help get the message across. Several concepts and techniques have already been covered in prior chapters from basic training documents to equipment use, from reference skills to other library services. Still, some staff training topics remain: basic desktop publishing principles, computer-based communications, speaking, slide shows, and videotaping.

Because communications takes in such a vast array of possibilities, librarians can match individual student staff interests and capabilities with a specific communications venue. As a results, less training needs to be done and higher quality products can be created. The approach can be as simple as showing staff examples of existing library communications and having them choose which ones to work on and improve. Students can also brainstorm new communications pieces as well and show their own designs for library consideration. Now that's good public relations!

Communications principles

Objectives:	The student will identify different communications media, stating the characteristics and advantages and disadvantages of each. The student will analyze and evaluate a variety of communication samples in terms of content and presentation. The student will determine the most appropriate medium to use to convey a specific idea.
Process:	The trainer explains the communications cycle. The trainer shows examples of different communications media, explaining its characteristics, advantages and disadvantages of each. The student analyzes existing communications pieces.

Demonstration ideas:
- Visit an advertising agency or mass media company.
- Brainstorm with the student about effective and ineffective communication.
- Start with a message and determine how it would be transmitted using different communications media.

Student activities:

Have the student
- Modify an existing communications piece.
- Collect and analyze examples of effective communication pieces, and analyze them.
- Trace a communications piece from idea to receiver's action, following the communications model.

Follow-up:

Link communications with other library services. Discuss the role of public relations in connection with communication. Talk about the effect of body language and other unconscious action in terms of communication.

Evaluation:

Can the student
- Trace a communications model?
- Identify different communications media, accurately stating the characteristics and advantages and disadvantages of each?
- Determine the most appropriate medium to use to convey a specific idea?
- Accurately analyze and evaluate a variety of communication samples in terms of content and presentation?

What's the Medium for the Message?

Each medium of communication has its advantages and disadvantages. Knowing which format best conveys your idea makes it easier to plan an effective message.

Written material is relatively easy to produce and modify, especially using computer software. If created in black and white, it is easy to reproduce and distribute widely. However, the content must be well written and designed so it will attract and be used by the reader.

Computer-based communications, such as Web pages or multimedia presentations, can seem glamorous to viewers. They send an underlying message that the library is state-of-the-art. Telecommunications can reach a global audience, so its impact can be significant. Multimedia provides a rich combination of sources that can be used by a variety of learning styles. The downside is that these products require much planning and design time and call for some sophisticated technical skills and equipment.

Speech, like the written word, is very flexible. Verbal communication may be in the form of an announcement, a report, a formal speech, a song, a skit or play, or an interview. The audience can be one to one million. Speakers are naturally more engaging because they are human; the audience is more likely to identify with a person than with a piece of paper. Speaking also carries a sense of immediacy and directness. However, one must also be wary of the spontaneous, unthinking statement that can cause undue embarrassment. Despite seeming "off the cuff," most speaking requires thoughtful preparation. And, unfortunately, even if the content is excellent, a poor presentation can undermine the entire message.

Slide shows have not been entirely replaced by video for several reasons: They can be easily rearranged and updated for different purposes, they have higher resolution, and they can be shown at different speeds. Of course, the slide show can be only as good as the slides themselves, so technical skill and an artistic eye are needed to produce a high-quality presentation. In addition, if sound is to be coordinated with the show, special equipment may be needed as well as extra time to program the machine.

Videotape has become a major communications medium. With its ability to capture live sound and motion, videotape immediately engages the audience visually and audibly. With editing capabilities, video can present a sophisticated collection of source material and sequence it dramatically. Moreover, because it can be duplicated and broadcast, videos can reach a side audience. The bad news? High-quality productions require hours and hours of time to plan, tape, edit, and reproduce. Relatively expensive equipment is needed, particularly for sophisticated productions, and technical expertise pretty much determines the results.

Steps in Planning a Communications Piece

1. Determine the need of the library and of the user.
2. Identify the most effective format.
3. Gather and structure the information.
4. Determine the "look" of the communication piece.
5. Transform the information to take best advantage of the chosen medium.

Further reading:
Barbara Conroy and Barbara Schindler Jones. *Improving Communication in the Library.* Oryx, 1986.

Desktop publishing (DTP) principles

Objectives:	The student will identify possible ways to communicate about the library through desktop publishing. The student will apply artistic and production principles when creating DTP documents.
Process:	The trainer will show examples of DTP documents and point out the artistic and production principles involved. The trainer will coach students as they analyze other DTP documents and as they modify an existing DTP document.
Demonstration ideas:	• Start with an idea and translate it into different DTP documents. • Visit a professional DTP service company. • Analyze a catalog of library promotion pieces and determine how they can be modified using the library's DTP resources.
Student activities:	Have the student • Compile and analyze effective DTP samples. • Modify an existing DTP document. • Compare different types of DTP documents.
Follow-up:	Link DTP with library publications such as bibliographies and reviews. Link DTP with other communication formats. Discuss how written documentation is included in major public relation campaigns.
Evaluation:	Can the student • Identify various types of desktop publishing documents? • Apply artistic and production principles effectively when creating DTP documents?

A Dozen Ways That the Library Can Use Desktop Publishing

Bookmarks: Create a library logo and list library hours on the strip.

Bibliographies: Develop annotated lists of summer reading fare.

Reviews: Incorporate scanned pictures from the book you are reviewing.

Fliers: Include a clip-off response slip on library video offers.

Posters: Use clip art "libraries" to jazz up library posters about the DDC.

Newsletters: Make library "news" with lists about new acquisitions, staff photos and interviews, book excerpts and computer screen dumps, reviews, word searches, search tips, hotline numbers, and more.

Stationary: Create a library DTP "look" with coordinated stationery.

Cards: Send student-designed and personalized thank you cards.

Postcards: Use heavy stock and fun graphics to mail announcements.

Business Cards: Design a library student staff card and personalize it.

Brochures: Produce tips for parents on reading encouragement.

Signs: Make 3D standing mini-signs about library rules.

Tips for Creating Great DTP Documents

The Basic Steps:
1. Create the text. Files can often be imported from other programs.
2. Create or input the graphics. Try scanning, clip art, paint programs.
3. Lay out the publication. Determine column and margin specifications, then arrange the text and artwork.
4. Proofread first, then print!

The Added Edge:
- Know your audience: students, teachers, parents.
- Know your message: Be clear, concise, and exciting. Spell correctly!
- Know your objective: Is it to educate, to persuade, to sell?
- Grab the person's attention! Use strong headlines, arresting graphics, dramatic use of space.
- Look "together": all DTP elements should be consistent and coordinated
- Use graphics effectively: Crop pictures for greatest impact, incorporate easy-to-read charts and graphs, accent with clip art.
- Break up space effectively: Use heads and subheads for easier reading; include sidebars and call-outs (boxed excerpts), reverse type, white space.

Further reading:
Roger C. Parker. *Looking Good in Print*. 3rd ed. Ventana, 1993.

Multimedia design principles

Objectives:	The student will identify characteristics of various multimedia products. The student will apply artistic and production principles when creating multimedia products.
Process:	The trainer will show examples of multimedia products and point out the artistic and production principles involved. The trainer will coach students as they analyze other multimedia products and as they modify an existing multimedia product.
Demonstration ideas:	• Visit a television studio to see how a show is put together. Alternatively, watch a video about the process. • "Take apart" a hypermedia product and analyze the use of graphics, links, transitions, and scripting. • Read source codes of Web pages and translate them into the final product.
Student activities:	Have the student • Analyze television shows in terms of artistic and production principles. • Choose a subject, gather information in various formats, and develop a plan to incorporate the sources into a multimedia product. • Modify an existing multimedia product.
Follow-up:	Link multimedia products with DTP and other communications means. Discuss how multimedia could be used for instruction or reader's advisory.
Evaluation:	Can the student • Identify characteristics of various multimedia products? • Transform library information into multimedia format accurately and efficiently? • Apply artistic and production principles effectively when creating multimedia products?

Promotion the Library Through Web Pages

First Impressions
Set the tone from the start: cozy? sophisticated? friendly? fast-paced?
Show the library name clearly and dramatically.
Pair the name with a professional-looking graphic, logo, or photo.
Give a classy "sound bite" about the library's mission.

Main menu
Show the variety of library services and resources using a short list of linked
options, which can refer to embedded "pages." Here are some ideas:

- Library orientation
- Library staff
- Library news
- Reviews and excerpts
- Readers' advisory
- In-house databases
- Subject guides with Internet sites
- Fun stuff: contests, trivia facts, question of the day, news-breaking
  info (award winners, sports scores.)

Design Considerations
Keep type simple. Use **boldface** and underlining sparingly.
Use color and texture for emphasis.
Watch margins and columns because screen sizes differ.
Look organized, not cluttered. Use graphical organizers, such as bars.

Further reading:
Paul McFedries. *Complete Idiot's Guide to Creating HTML Web Pages.*
  Que, 1996.

Developing Multimedia Projects

Plan!
What's the objective?
Who's the audience?
What's the content?
What are the "look" and tone?
What are the parameters: size limits, deadline, costs?

Organize!
Create a storyboard, flow chart or outline of the project. One good practice is to create an index card (or larger) for each screen; in that way, screens can be easily rearranged.

Gather the source material: text, sound, graphics, video. (Write down the citation for each source in case it needs to be credited.)

Incorporate the sources into the storyboard and modify as needed.

Take advantage of multimedia features to add pizazz and interaction: non-linearity, links, pop-up fields, options for comments, test or other feedback features.

Have one person act as manager to keep everything organized.

Have one person act as key technician to insure a consistent look.

Further reading:
Marianne G. Handler, Ann S. Dana and Jane Peters Moore. *Hypermedia as a Student Tool.* Libraries Unlimited, 1995.

Michelle Robinette. *Mac Multimedia for Teachers.* IDG, 1995.

W. Thomas Walker and Paula K. Montgomery. *Media Production and Computer Activities.* ABC-CLIO, 1990.

Speaking techniques

Objectives: The student will identify different ways that speaking skills can be used to communicate about the library. The student wil identify key elements of effective speech. The student will apply good speaking techniques when communicating about the library.

Process: The trainer demonstrates effective speaking practice. The trainer and student develop a list of key ingredients to good speaking. The student practices those techniques, and the trainer coaches as needed. The student and trainer develop a list of possible library public relations activities that include speaking skills.

Demonstration ideas:
- Watch professional speakers and analyze their speech patterns and practices. Listen to professional speakers and analyze their techniques.
- Have a drama teacher or public speaker demonstrate good speaking techniques.
- List different speaking activities and compare them in terms of speaking skills.

Student activities: Have the student
- Act out effective and ineffective speaking techniques.
- Choose effective speaking role models from television and tape their speeches.
- Attend a dramatic production and analyze it relative to speaking techniques.

Follow-up: Link speaking skills to communications within the library: at the desk, doing readers' advisory. Discuss how speaking skills influence interpersonal skills. Compare speaking and writing skills.

Evaluation: Can the student
- Identify different ways that speaking skills can be used to communicate about the library?
- Identify key elements of effective speech?
- Apply good speaking techniques when communicating about the library?
- Participate competently in some form of speaking activity for the library, such as public announcements, presentations for groups, skits, readings, interviewing, creating audiotapes?

Public Speaking Guidelines

The Basics

Be prepared! Know your subject and your audience. Practice.

Be on time. If using equipment, try to test it ahead of time.

Be friendly. Smile.

Be natural. Dress appropriately and comfortably. Maintain good posture.

Be enthusiastic and sincere.

Start strong. Memorize your opening lines. Make a good first impression.

Speak in a relaxed way, don't speak too fast or too slowly. Pause when it's appropriate.

Speak clearly and loudly enough.

Modulate your voice to make a point; use gestures sparingly.

Close strongly. Memorize your closing lines. Make a good last impression.

Know when to stop talking. Stop.

How To Overcome Stage Fright

Acknowledge your fears. Turn around the fear and think of it as an energizer.

Practice, practice, practice. Practice in front of a full-length mirror, in front of a person, in front of a video camera.

Super-prepare the first five minutes of your speech.

Talk about things that are important to you and that you enjoy.

Be centered. You're the expert, so show your enthusiasm!

Get to know the site ahead of time.

Pace yourself so you will arrive at the site in plenty of time.

Get to the site refreshed and relaxed. Don't drink caffeine just before the speech.

Visualize your success. Close your eyes, breathe slowly and deeply, and visualize the end of the speech and the warm applause. Then open your eyes and get set to give the greatest speech of your life!

Further reading:

Steve Bareham. "Improve Your Public Speaking," *Emergency Librarian.* Sept., 1988.

Curt Simmons. *Public Speaking Made Simple.* Made Simple, 1996.

Slide show techniques

Objectives:
The student will identify the characteristics of a well-designed slide show. The student will help plan and produce a slide show.

Process:
The trainer presents a slide show and explains the features of a good product. The trainer traces the planning steps in creating a slide show. The trainer coaches students as they develop a slide show.

Demonstration ideas:
- Analyze photographs and illustrations that would make good slide material.
- Compare a slide show to a photo album or pictorial book.
- Have a professional photographer give tips on creating slide shows.

Student activities:
Have the student
- Create a slide show storyboard.
- Choose a subject, and select visuals or take photographs for a slide show.
- Analyze a professional slide show or television program that resembles a slide show.
- Rearrange existing slides to create an original show.

Follow-up:
Link slide shows to videotape productions and multimedia presentations. Discuss visual literacy attributes. Compare visual, written, and oral communication.

Evaluation:
Can the student
- Identify the characteristics of a well-designed slide show?
- Effectively apply design and production principles when creating a slide show?
- Effectively plan and produce a slide show?

Tips for Creating Super Slide Shows

Plan
Know the objective.
Know the subject.
Know the audience.
Create the show on paper using a storyboard or individual index cards.
Gather the source material.
Always have a loaded camera handy

Using Text
Show one idea per slide, preferably with a visual cue.
Use six or fewer lines of text per slide.
Link size and color to importance: The bigger the type, the more important
    the idea. Print the key word in a contrasting color.
Use simple, sans serif typeface. Block letters are best.
Use upper and lower case letters; ALL CAPITALS are hard to read.

Using Images
Take lots of pictures. Vary the exposure and the cropping.
Avoid using flash; use high-speed film instead.
Avoid posed shots of people; they'll look frozen.
Create a unified look for the show.
Use a library logo to identify the slide show.
Use color selectively; follow a color scheme, such as earth colors.
Contrast text with the background color; black on yellow is best.
Make sure the image is clear and crisp (though-out-of-focus pictures can be
    used to demonstrate vagueness, poor vision).

Sequencing
Start and end with a black slide.
The first visible slide should be the title.
The second slide (or the last visible one) should be the credits.
Number the slides in case they get dropped. You can also draw a diagonal
    line across the top of the slide series as an easy visual cue.

Further reading:
Ron Slawson. *Multi-image Slide/tape Programs*. Libraries Unlimited, 1988.

Videotape techniques

Objectives: The student will identify the characteristics of a well-designed videotape production. The student will help plan and produce a videotape.

Process: The trainer presents a video and explains the features of a good production. The trainer traces the planning steps in creating a video production. The trainer coaches the students as they develop a video production.

Demonstration ideas:
- Analyze television productions in terms of technical aspects.
- Have a professional video producer trace the steps of developing a video production.
- Work backwards from a finished video to the original idea.

Student activities: Have the student
- Create a video storyboard.
- Tape a television advertisement or short segment and re-edit it.
- Tape several news clips and edit them into a video production.

Follow-up: Discuss how video selection and editing changes the perspective and tone of a videotape. Compare video productions to slide shows and multimedia presentations. Discuss possible uses of videotapes to enhance library service or publicize the library.

Evaluation: Can the student
- Identify the characteristics of a well-designed videotape production?
- Apply sound production and design principles when creating a video production?
- Effectively help plan and produce a videotape?

Steps in Developing a Videotape Production

1. Get the Idea
What is the objective?
What is the message?
Who is the audience?
What's the best way to convey the message?

2. Get the Crew
Producer: coordinates the crew
Director: calls the shots
Camera crew: videotapes the program
Sound engineer: controls the audio portion
Floor manager: using the script, gets all props and equipment ready and
    signals talent or crew
Anchor: person who hosts a show; often the interviewer
Editor: makes the final cuts and sequences; usually creates special effects
    and transitions; incorporates text

3. Write the Script or Storyboard
Include both visual and audio components.
Time each sequence.
Write clearly, simply, and concisely.
Remember: *action*; don't tell, *show*.

4. Create the Visuals
All title cards or other signs should be 3/4 landscape ratio:
Ideally, use dark block letters on light gray background.
Have no more than six lines of text.
Letters should be at least one inch high.

5. Videotape
Keep the site quiet, especially near the camera.
Use appropriate lighting, and key the camera to it.
Rehearse the talent.
Keep the camera steady, unless you want to give a sense of dizziness.
Keep in focus, unless you want to give a fuzzy impression.
Vary the shots.
Compose the shots carefully.
  • Crop people at the knee or chest.
  • Keep a little space above the head.
  • Show visual space ahead of walking direction.
  • Shoot people at an angle to give perspective.
When in doubt, reshoot.

6. Edit

Review all tapes, and write the VCR counter number at the point that each
   segment begins.

Select and review any outside audio sources.

Write the editing script before the actual mechanical editing starts.

"Black" a clean master tape so you can assembly- or insert-edit.

Preview each edit before making the permanent edit.

When done, break off the videotape box "tabs" to prevent any overtaping.

KEEP THE MASTER IN A SAFE PLACE!

Further reading:

Augie Beasley. *Looking Great With Video*. Linworth Publishing, 1994.

Virginia Wallace and Ramona Gorham. *School News Shows; Video Production with a Focus*. Linworth Publishing, 1996.

Bibliography

American Association of School Librarians and Association for Educational Communications and Technology, *Information Power: Guidelines for School Library Media Programs*. AASL and AECT, 1988.

Mary Alice Anderson, *Teaching Information Literacy Using Electronic Resources for Grades 6-12*. Linworth Publishing, 1996.

David A. Baldwin, *Supervising Student Employees in Academic Libraries: A Handbook*. Libraries Unlimited, 1991.

Steve Bareham, "Improve Your Public Speaking," *Emergency Librarian*. Sept. 1988.

Diana Barnett, *Everything You Need to Know About the School Library Media Center: A Handbook for LMC Aides*. Alleyside Press, 1995.

Anne E. Barron and Karen S. Ivers, *The Internet and Instruction: Activities and Ideas*. Libraries Unlimited, 1996.

Caroline Feller Bauer, *Caroline Feller Bauer's New Handbook for Storytellers*. American Library Association, 1993.

Augie Beasley, *Looking Great With Video*. Linworth Publishing, 1994.

Joni Richards Bodart, *Booktalker's Companion*. Bookhooks Press, 1995.

Katharine Toch Bucher, *Computers and Technology in School Library Media Centers*. Linworth Publishing, 1994.

Christy C. Bulkeley, editor, *Media Resource Guide: How to Tell Your Story*. 4th ed. Foundation for American Communications, 1985.

Barbara Conroy and Barbara Schindler Jones, *Improving Communication in the Library*. Oryx, 1986.

Richard L. Curwin and Alen N. Mendler, *Discipline with Dignity*. Association for Supervision and Curriculum Development, 1988.

Donna W. Dalton, "How to Train and Evaluate Student Media Assistants," *Technology Connection*. Oct. 1994.

Don Dinkmeyer and Gary D. McKay, *Parenting Teenagers*. 2nd ed. American Guidance Service, 1990.

Arden Druce, *Complete Library Skills Activities Program*. The Center for Applied Research in Education, 1990.

Lesley S. J. Farmer, *Cooperative Learning Activities in the Library Media Center*. Libraries Unlimited, 1991.

Lesley S. J. Farmer, *Creative Partnerships: Librarians and Teachers Working Together*. Linworth Publishing, 1993.

Lesley S. J. Farmer, *Leadership Within the School Library and Beyond*. Linworth Publishing, 1994.

Lesley S. J. Farmer, *Workshops for Teachers: Becoming Partners for Information Literacy*. Linworth Publishing, 1995.

Gaylord Preservation Pathfinders. Gaylord Bros., 1995.

Marianne G. Handler, Ann D. Dana and Jane Peters Moore, *Hypermedia as a Student Tool*. Libraries Unlimited, 1995.

David W. and Frank P. Johnson, *Joining Together: Group Theory and Group Skills*. 5th ed. Prentice-Hall, 1994.

Lesley Kamenshine, *A-V Troubleshooting: Audio-Visual Equipment Operation, Maintenance, and Repair*. Prentice-Hall, 1985.

William A. Katz, *Introduction to Reference Work*. 6th ed. McGraw-Hill, 1991.

Pat Lang, *Introduction to Telecommunications*. Marin County of Education, 1995.

Kathy Howard Latrobe and Mildred Knight Laughlin, *Multicultural Aspects of Library Media Programs*. Libraries Unlimited, 1992.

Rena B. Lewis and Donald H. Doorlag, *Teaching Special Students in the Mainstream*. 2nd ed. Merrill Publishing, 1987.

Phyllis B. Leonard, *Choose, Use, Enjoy, Share: Library Media Skills for the Gifted Child*. Libraries Unlimited, 1985.

Paul McFedries, *Complete Idiot's Guide to Creating Html Web Pages*. Que, 1996.

Jane Nelson, *Positive Discipline*. Ballantine, 1987.

Esther Onishi and Erica Peto, "Training Students as Technology Assistants," *Technology Connection*. May 1996.

Marjorie Pappas, "Generic Instructions for Electronic Resources," *Technology Connection*. March 1994.

Roger C. Parker, *Looking Good in Print.* 3rd ed. Ventana, 1993.

Toni Pray, *Lessons for the Library Student Staff.* Linworth Publishing, 1992.
Margaret Y. Rabb, *Presentation Design Book.* Ventana, 1993.

Sally Gardner Reed, *Library Volunteers—Worth the Effort! A Program Manager's Guide.* McFarland, 1994.

Michelle Robinette, *Mac Multimedia for Teachers.* IDG Books, 1995.

Curt Simmons, *Public Speaking Made Simple.* Made Simple, 1996.

Ron Slawson, *Multi-image Slide/tape Programs.* Libraries Unlimited, 1988.

Karen G. Schneider, *The Internet Access Cookbook; A Librarian's Commonsense Guide to Low-Cost Connections.* Neal-Schuman, 1996.

Suzy Turner, *Biography Stack Template.* Mississippi State University Library, 1992.

U. S. Department of Education. College Library Technology and Cooperation. *Computer-based Library Instruction Project.* Washington, DC, 1994.

H. Thomas Walker and Paula K. Montgomery, *Media Production and Computer Activities.* ABC-CLIO, 1990.

Virginia Wallace and Ramona Gorham, *School News Shows; Video Production with a Focus.* Linworth Publishing, 1996.

Alice H. Yucht, *The Elementary School Librarian's Desk Reference: Library Skills and Management.* Linworth Publishing, 1992.